An Illustrated History of The National Physical Laboratory

A Century of Measurement

Eileen Magnello
(with editorial advice from Graeme Gooday)

To the memory of my brothers
Brian Magnello (1956-1976) and
Howard Magnello (1949-1989)
who studied and taught physics
and engineering, and were
fascinated by problems of
measurement for physical constants

First published in 2000
Canopus Publishing Limited
48 Cranwells Park
Bath BA1 2YE, UK

A catalogue record for this book is available from the British Library

ISBN 0 9537868 1 1

Designed and typeset by Malcolm Manning

Printed and bound in Great Britain by the University Press, Cambridge

CONTENTS

ACKNOWLEDGEMENTS

A number of people have provided much valuable assistance in the course of writing this book. I would like to thank firstly NPL library staff who helped to find material and photocopied reams of documents. In this regard, I should especially like to thank Sue Osborne who read several versions of this book, located a substantial amount of material and compiled the index. Margaret Jones assisted in locating a number of NPL photographs. The archivists at the Royal Society and the PRO also helped me find a number of documents. Former and current NPL directors and deputy directors, including Peter Campion, Paul Dean, Peter Clapham, John Rae and Andrew Wallard gave interviews and provided much useful material. I am particularly grateful to Peter Clapham who read the final version of the manuscript, clarified a number of issues and offered much valuable advice. A number of former NPL scientists gave me much useful material about their time at NPL, including Roger Townsend, Walter Vickers, John Gates and Alan Jennings in addition to all those scientists from the Glazebrook Association who wrote to me about their times at NPL.

I am also grateful to a number of friends and colleagues for their assistance and advice. Graeme Gooday gave much scholarly support on a number of matters relating to the historical context of physics laboratories and measurement while Mary Croacken's suggestions for *Chapter 15* on "Computers at the NPL" were much appreciated. Peter Bell, Elsbeth Heaman, Lois Reynolds and Cassie Watson edited and proof-read different versions of the text and shared their criticisms and thoughts with me. Special thanks are extended to the Academic Unit of the Wellcome Trust who provided me with essential office space and computers for the project, and to Roy Porter who first brought it to my attention that NPL was looking for someone to write its centenary history.

PREFACE

As the outgoing director of the National Physical Laboratory, I am very pleased to welcome this new history of NPL. When I arrived as director about four years ago, I was immediately struck by the mix of history and twenty-first century science which pervades NPL and makes it so fascinating on many levels.

The first director, Richard Tetley Glazebrook, was appointed on January 1st 1900 and NPL was established shortly afterwards at Bushy House – by then over 200 years old with a colourful history of its own. It is still used as a laboratory and, in some respects, a very good one. There are several other listed historical buildings in NPL's grounds and some very old trees including a sweet chestnut dating back to about 1360. Other buildings, in regular use, date back to the early 1900s lending their own historical perspective. Inside these buildings are some of the country's brightest scientists and engineers working at the frontiers of their fields: measuring time to better than a millionth of a millionth of a second; defects in optical fibres kilometres long; or detailed properties of individual trapped atoms.

During its 100 years, NPL has seen many changes. Time and again it has taken up development of some new science or technology for the benefit of Britain. At appropriate stages these key projects have been passed on to more specialised laboratories or to industry only to be replaced by new priorities. Radio, aeronautics, ship design, radar, computing, and quantum metrology are some examples.

The role and the character of NPL are still changing and must do so. My arrival in 1995 happened because the private company Serco Group plc won the contract to manage NPL on behalf of the British government. Overnight NPL's staff ceased to be scientific civil servants of the Department of Trade and Industry and joined the private sector. There were many other consequential changes, some profound, but I believe, mostly beneficial. Even more recently construction has begun of a new state-of-the-art laboratory building which in 2002 will house, for the first time in its history, the whole of NPL under one roof. So we will take another significant step forward.

This book is intended to mark NPL's centenary by telling some of the story. I wish you pleasure in reading it.

Dr John Rae, Managing Director (1995–2000)

FOREWORD

It is a little over 30 years since I first walked through the gates of NPL as a member of staff and, at the time, it was one of the greatest thrills of my life. The thrill remains.

Why has metrology captivated so many of us over the years? It's a strange sort of science to pursue for most, if not all, of a working life. Is it because the experiments are all at the cutting edge of science and are intrinsically so long term? Is it because there is innate satisfaction in "getting the right answer"? Is it because of the international camaraderie and collaboration which is both implicit and essential to success?

The answer is that it's a combination of all of these, and much more. My own experience started a little before I joined the permanent staff and mainly because I had the good fortune to have the charismatic Arthur Maitland as a new optics lecturer at the University of St Andrews. We had built one of the first lasers ever to operate in Britain and, as a result, he arranged for me to spend a summer as a vacation student in one of the new laser groups at NPL. I was hooked from that moment on. The place was a magnet for creative people with sparkling ideas: Essen, Froome, Cook, Wilkinson, Davies, Gebbie, Pople, Turing, "big" Jim Burch, Hondros, and Dyson – these names were world famous and they followed a long tradition of similar achievers. And here we were, mingling with them over lunch or coffee, raw young scientists with so much to learn, particularly about the hard work and discipline of metrology. With all the naiveté of the young idealist, big dreams born of Wednesday afternoon practicals overlooking the North Sea, I was sure that my new project on stabilised lasers was going to take all of a few months to finish. Ten years on and we were just about there, but we knew that we were right and that the international metrology world could achieve similar performance. We also came to realise that there were no quick fixes: it was to be another seven years before the realisation of the metre using laser light was adopted internationally!

Metrology is a long-term business where international co-operation and pooled ideas lie at the heart of all we are striving to achieve. The metrologist must work in a spirit of mutual co-operation, but he – and increasingly she, thank goodness – also responds vitally to the stimulus of that competitive instinct to publish first. We at NPL have the best of all possible worlds: purpose, tradition, the opportunity for personal achievement and the knowledge that the results of our work are of direct benefit to a whole range of industrial, scientific and social users.

NPL's beginnings stemmed from the need to serve the demands of practical industrial measurement and to underpin "well made" products. It started with only three departments – Engineering, Physics and an Observatory Department – but soon mushroomed as anyone who has visited the Teddington site can see all too clearly. The Aerodynamics, Electricity and Metrology Departments were set up after the First World War. Radio and Light Departments were added in the 1930s and 1940s by which time the laboratory was responsible for nearly all of the tests and calibrations in the country; thousands of gauge blocks, thermometers, resistors and clocks also came through those gates for calibration.

The late 1960s and 1970s saw the creation of new divisions to tackle molecular science and the emerging techniques of "autonomics". NPL, at its largest then, was the place for national challenges, adding to, and sustaining, a fine and proud history of world firsts: radar; digital computing; atomic clocks; light emitting polymers; and the world's first "local area network" which truly was the earliest Internet. Much of this work has now, rightly, passed to others, but our tradition and heritage are still very much alive. We have returned to our roots, a measurement laboratory, but one which has completely changed its way of working with industry. The birth of the British Calibration Service in 1965 – another NPL first – was intended to transfer routine measurement to the private sector, relieving NPL of a huge calibration load and also stimulating greater appreciation of the relevance to companies of measurement. It also made room for NPL to tackle new areas such as acoustics and the environment. If Glazebrook, Rosenhain or Petavel were able to visit us today they would recognise much the same spirit of scientific excitement and challenge as they once nurtured but they would be amazed, I am sure, at our scope and precision.

This book deals as much with the present as well as the past leaving us well aware of the importance of continuity and reputation. As for the future, we can safely predict a growing need for measurement in a whole range of new areas in an institution, in the best sense of that word, which is the perfect national focus for it. NPL has been good at adapting to the external environment, political as well as technical, and there is every reason for it to do so in the next millennium.

At the heart of what we do is the seemingly simple but, practically and technically, demanding notion of traceable measurement. We shall always be pressing our knowledge of physics and chemistry to their limits; that is our job. That is also why new science is so often first applied to metrology giving it an association with a string of Nobel prize-winners – Josephson, Ramsay, Schalow, Townes, and Phillips to name but a few.

There is charm as well as intellectual challenge, in pushing forward the boundaries of metrology: those who follow us through the gates of NPL will, I hope, share the excitement of, as well as our pride in, a fine and famous place.

Andrew Wallard, Deputy Director (1990–)

Introduction

The first century of the National Physical Laboratory (NPL) has been an eventful one. Its directors and staff have had to manage its daily work and long term research in at least four major different areas of activity: the maintenance and refinement of measurement standards (metrology); commercial testing for British industry; the conduct of innovative scientific research, and the improvement of new technologies. If one *leitmotif* in this centenary history is the persistent challenge of fulfiling these roles in radically varying socio-economic circumstances, another is the often vexed question of the legitimacy of using state funds to support scientific research. During the life-time of NPL, this has often been a delicate matter for scientists and the public, not least because throughout its history the bulk of NPL's funding came from government sources until 1995 when NPL became a government owned and contractor operated (GOCO) organisation.

Although this is a study of a "national" laboratory, it is also essential to understand the history of NPL within the international contexts of industrial competition and scientific collaboration. It can plausibly be argued that NPL was established in response to the opening of the Physikalisch Technische Reichsanstalt (PTR) in the outskirts of Berlin in 1887, and that its early form mirrored the activities of its German counterpart. The early NPL followed the pattern of the PTR with its fundamental emphasis on metrological work as a state repository of standards and calibration procedures, growing soon to be a place where innovative research was undertaken. Moreover, the staff at NPL were fortunate to learn from the fraught experiences of the PTR that it was prudent not to locate a sophisticated standards laboratory within range of the electromagnetic disturbances of city tram lines!

When Sir Richard Tetley Glazebrook was appointed the first director on January 1st 1900, the Laboratory (which opened its doors in 1902) became the first government-funded institution in Britain to undertake both scientific research and to provide services for industry. The Treasury's decision to provide funding for such research as could benefit manufacturing industries throughout Britain, heralded the beginning of a new level of commitment by the government to scientific affairs. Nevertheless, scientists have often claimed, rightly or wrongly, that however much money they received, it was not enough. Whatever the case may be, the recurrent commitment of successive governments to the economic and military importance of scientific research represented a significant move away from the Victorian *laissez faire* attitude which maintained that industrial activities should be the exclusive domain of private enterprise. This level of government commitment to the work of NPL was especially apparent during the two global conflicts of the twentieth century at which time the funding and fortunes of NPL waxed greatly – ironically waning during the peacetime years.

During the First World War, British scientists felt they had established a sound case for public commitment to applied scientific research, and it was the Department of Scientific and Industrial Research (DSIR), created in 1916, which managed the Laboratory for 43 years. Following the development of radar and nuclear weapons during Second World War and Britain's testing of its first atomic bomb in 1952, NPL underwent major reorientation and reorganisation in the 1950s, accompanied by many other technological developments of the so-called "Cold War". The decade after 1945 brought about Britain's first programmable electronic computer (the ACE machine) and developments in molecular science and quantum physics. Then with the introduction of the caesium atomic-beam to measure time, NPL became the nation's timekeeper (a role filled originally by Greenwich Observatory). The 1960s heralded the growth of "Big Science" and the "white heat of technology", stimulating the rapid growth of atomic energy, molecular science, computers and weapons technologies. Despite these changes, the DSIR became aware that the distribution between applied research and basic research was problematic due to the recurrent scarcity of important resources demanded by all researchers. Following the conclusions from the Trend Report in 1962, which drew attention to the speed and growth of organised science since the end of the First World War, Harold Wilson's Labour government disbanded the DSIR and set up a Ministry of Technology in 1964. The search for a well-defined industrial role continued under successive governments during the 1960s and early 1970s. The ministry managed NPL until 1971 when it was transferred to the Department of Trade and Industry (DTI) after the Conservative government returned to power.

During the 1980s the political trend towards privatisation, and the end of large-scale military research for the Cold War, brought profound changes to the infrastructure of NPL. Under the Conservative government's "Next Steps Initiative", NPL was formally vested as an executive agency of the DTI on July 3rd 1990. In the following year a substantial programme for refurbishing and rebuilding the Laboratory had begun. After NPL became a government-owned and contractor-operated (GOCO) organisation on October 1st 1995, the DTI still retained the ownership of the buildings and the major equipment of NPL and was its largest customer. Contractorisation changed the balance of the work and this has given NPL longer term planning and more freedom to manage under the GOCO arrangement. Various companies and consortia were invited to bid for the project management and the five-year contract was awarded to Serco Group plc on July 13th 1995; its contract was recently extended by two years and is now due to expire in 2002. A decision was made in 1996 by the DTI to build a new multi-purpose Laboratory occupying 36,000 square metres under a private finance initiative.

Even before this new suite of laboratories, workshops and offices are ready for occupation (expected in 2002), one of the newest tools that is expected to facilitate changes in NPL's commercial role is the use of the Internet for remote electrical calibration of instruments. The historians who write the volume to celebrate the second centenary of NPL at the end of the twenty-first century will doubtless have much to say about the accuracy of that prediction.

CHAPTER 1

Early Proposals for State Laboratories

The First Lord and the Chancellor of the Exchequer recommend to the Board that a Committee should be appointed: to consider and report upon the desirability of establishing a National Physical Laboratory for the testing and verification of instruments for physical investigation: for the construction and preservation of standards of measurement: and for the systematic determination of physical constants and numerical data useful for scientific and industrial purposes; and to report whether the work of such an institution, if established, could be associated with any testing or standardizing work already performed wholly or partly at the public cost.

Treasury Minutes of the National Physical Laboratory, August 3rd 1897.

During the first two thirds of the nineteenth century, almost all scientific activity in Britain was maintained by private organisations and supported financially by philanthropy and/or commercial fee-paying operations. As examples of this 'voluntarist' science, London boasted the Royal Society and the Royal Institution (founded 1799) and both mechanics institutes and literary and philosophical societies also flourished in many parts of the country. At University College (founded 1826) and King's College (founded 1828), scientific research was nurtured in London without government support, and the British Association for the Advancement of Science (BAAS) was founded as a peripatetic national forum for publicising such research in 1831. In this context, Charles Babbage's contemporary complaint that England's science had fallen into 'decline' relative to that of France and Germany, should be seen specifically as an attack on the Royal Society for allowing a predominance of research-inactive aristocrats among its fellows.

Babbage and others made intermittent but vociferous calls for

Lieutenant-Colonel Alexander Strange. By courtesy of the National Portrait Gallery, London.

government support to restore the vitality of native research, but state support was generally granted only to educational institutions in the capital: the Royal College of Chemistry (1845) and the School of Mines (1851), as well as the government's own Department of Science and Art (1853). Successive administrations inclined to the view that if scientific investigation were needed, it would surely pay for itself by its economic benefits. This *laissez-faire* attitude towards science was borne out by the results of the Great Exhibition in 1851: British commerce and manufacturing enjoyed undisputed world leadership in most areas of industry, despite the minimal investment of state resources in such enterprise. This leadership continued unchallenged for over a decade and a half, even while continental manufacturers began to develop systems of scientific education for industry.

The first serious debate about the role of science in British industry took place in response to the Paris International Exhibition of 1867 at which continental manufacturers won a significantly larger proportion of the prizes than at previous exhibitions. Although many of the finest examples of British industry were not represented, notably the 1866 Atlantic telegraph cable, many agreed that the evidence presented at Paris showed that unless Britain introduced more advanced education for its industrial workers and experts, it was eventually bound to be eclipsed by competitor nations. In response to this threat the Liberal government of 1870 enacted a scheme of universal primary education to promote a minimum literacy and numeracy in its workforce. More tellingly, however, industrial communities across the country – notably in Leeds, Birmingham and Sheffield – sponsored the creation of their own new civic colleges (later universities), with little support from the government, soon developing their own facilities for laboratory research.

By 1869, the Board of Trade founded a Standards Laboratory which was housed in the Jewel Tower, Old Palace Yard, Westminster, to provide the relevant testing and calibration facilities for the newly enacted standards. While state and civic support for scientific education was won relatively easily in the 1870s, the case for similar support for scientific research was much harder to prove. In the wake of the Paris International Exhibition of 1867, the BAAS launched a campaign for the state sponsorship of scientific careers. One of the earliest advocates of a new relationship between government and science was Lieutenant-Colonel Alexander Strange, an ex-Indian Army Officer and amateur astronomer, who was one of the judges at the Paris Exhibition. At the BAAS meeting of 1868 in Norwich, Strange put forward his view that adequate progress in physical science in Britain could only be secured by government involvement, especially given the large amount of capital needed to supply buildings and costly appliances.

This campaign for the endowment of science found an ally in the journal *Nature* (founded 1869) which soon became the leading British journal promoting the interests of scientists. Even in its early issues, it lobbied for an enquiry into the state of science in Britain. The journal's editor, Norman Lockyer, drew attention to the involvement of the German government in promoting science, noting that Britain had resources and talent of the same order as Germany, but lacked government help. Lockyer accordingly argued that a minister of science should be appointed with a council to advise the government on matters relating to science and industry.

The Devonshire Commission

Lockyer's campaign did not go unnoticed. By February 1870, the Liberal Prime Minister William Gladstone agreed to appoint a royal commission under William Cavendish, Seventh Duke of Devonshire, to study the existing national provision for scientific instruction and the advancement of science. The Devonshire Commission sat for six years, met 85 times and interviewed more than 150 witnesses with Lockyer himself acting as its secretary. Although the commission looked mainly at scientific instruction in schools, museums and universities, it also raised penetrating questions about the state of British science in general, and about research in particular. A committee was formed for the purpose of determining if there was sufficient justification in Great Britain and Ireland to undertake research in the physical sciences.[1]

Soon after Lockyer was made secretary to the Royal Commission, a series of articles appeared in *Nature* in 1871 on the endowment of research. These articles advocated state intervention, promoting the still somewhat contentious view that national progress depended essentially on scientific research. The allegedly distressed state of scientific men became well known, and invidious, if highly selective, comparisons with the situation in Germany became commonplace. This comparison was especially telling since unification of the German State in the wake of the Franco-Prussian War had created a strong new economic and industrial power in Europe, and the great expansion of industry in Germany saw considerable collaboration with the scientific community. Scientists in the *Nature* lobby complained that, unlike the German state, the British government did "next to nothing" for the promotion of science; moreover, it provided no careers for science students in Britain. The journal even alleged that true scientific research was "absolutely unencouraged and unpaid", and suggested instead that government aid could be financed by an additional tax that would be repaid to the country through improved living conditions.

Lockyer's persistence and the testimony of sympathetic witnesses from the scientific community succeeded in persuading the Devonshire

Lord Kelvin with his brother James Thomson and sister, Elizabeth King by Agnes Gardner King. By courtesy of the National Portrait Gallery, London.

Commission that government aid was essential to the future of science, particularly by the establishment of public laboratories.[2] In its eighth report of 1874, the commission recommended that a national technical laboratory and physical observatory be built. Although the scientific lobby had the support of a Royal Commission, the Liberal government of the day would not commit itself to such a costly state intervention, nor acquiesce in what many saw as self-interested claims for finance that were only certain to benefit the scientists themselves. The government preferred instead to encourage universities and colleges by discretionary grants, leaving individual industries to invest selectively in technical education ventures. Indeed it was Gladstone's personal exhortations to the ancient merchant companies that led them to return to their long neglected responsibilities and introduce the City and Guilds examination schemes by the end of the decade.

Although the Devonshire Commission of 1874 had proposed the establishment of national laboratories, Sir William Thomson (later Lord Kelvin) had made similar suggestions in 1871 at the BAAS meeting. At this meeting, Thomson expressed his regret that the British government confined its support to educational measures rather than by the direct sponsorship of research. In the early 1870s there were a few physical laboratories in Britain, and those were usually attached to universities including Edinburgh, Owens College, Manchester and Glasgow (where Thomson had set up his physics laboratory). Thomson, however, believed that university laboratories alone could not provide for the needs of the nation.

The continued prevalence of *laissez-faire* policies was apparent in the establishment of the Marine Biological Association (MBA) in 1884 and a laboratory built in Plymouth in the following year.[3] Though the government contributed some funds to building the MBA laboratory at Plymouth, most of the funding was raised by private donations, and especially by the Victorian marine biologist, E Ray Lankester. Yet changes in economic conditions during the last two decades of the nineteenth century led to other changes in the way that the British government and population perceived the relationship between science and industry. Victorian prosperity had reached its peak in 1873, and by the 1890s British manufacturers were starting to feel keen competition particularly from American and German industries. They thus began to scrutinise the educational schemes, industrial infrastructure and governmental roles in both Germany and the United States to discover ways of increasing their own productivity. The German government awarded grants for various types of industrial research to such an extent that the German dye industry and the Jena Glass industry achieved virtual world monopolies. In 1887 the productive union of German science with industry was epitomised by the opening of the state testing and research institute known as the Physikalisch Technische Reichsanstalt (PTR) constructed in Charlottenburg, a Berlin suburb, in the preceding four years. Hermann von Helmholtz was its first director and Werner von Siemens was one of its main industrial supporters.

At the same time, the technical schools in the United States were offering specialised education to students who were preparing to enter industry just as Britain's technical colleges were doing in London, Manchester and other manufacturing centres – also without state assistance. Nevertheless, as the rationale for *laissez-faire* diminished in the face of unfavourable results from fierce international competition, the British government began slowly to respond more favourably towards funding British science, although not everyone in Britain believed that investment in scientific research was necessary or even sufficient to alleviate the condition of national industry.

Proposals for British standards laboratories

The growth of laboratory research in British colleges and universities throughout the 1880s did, however, make it difficult to argue that there was any need for the state to pay for careers in scientific research. Strange's vision of 1884 was still unfulfilled. Yet with the growth in the electrical lighting industry, there were new calls instead for the foundation of a state laboratory that had special responsibility for calibrating electrical instruments to legal measurement standards. In 1885, while

Richard Tetley Glazebrook.

the PTR was under construction in Berlin, John Ambrose Fleming put just such a proposal to the Society of Telegraph Engineers and Electricians (later the Institution for Electrical Engineers). As Edward Pyatt has observed, Fleming emphatically did not seek state funding for this laboratory, arguing instead that it could be paid for through the fees accruing from the many thousands of electrical patents submitted each year.[4] Although there was no immediate response to Fleming's idea, five years later the government appointed a Board of Trade committee to consider a legislative basis for electrical measurement standards.

In 1889, an appeal for financial support for such a laboratory was made by prominent members of the electrical profession and the Board of Trade agreed to this soon after. The laboratory was set up in six rooms in the basement of 8 Richmond Terrace, Whitehall. Between 1891 and 1894 this laboratory determined the practical electrical standards required by the relevant 1889 legislation on electrical measurement. By August 1894 these standards were implemented in further legislation. The sole purposes of this laboratory were: to obtain and preserve standards for the measurement of electrical quantities; to give the standard measurements of those quantities; and to enable the electrical adviser of the Board of Trade to make such tests of instruments and material as would be necessary for the performance of his duties. No scientific work outside these purposes was to be undertaken.

Yet this move forward was still not enough for the scientists who wanted an establishment much more akin to that of the PTR in Germany. In 1891, the Liverpool physicist Oliver Lodge addressed the concerns for the establishment of a national physical laboratory in his presidential address to the BAAS at Cardiff. Lodge drew attention to the work at the Reichsanstalt, claiming that the progress in physical science in Britain was somewhat haphazard and even pursued in an "amateur" fashion. Accordingly, he appealed for the establishment of a national physical laboratory at which, under suitable direction, a group of workers could undertake accurate determinations of physical constants for electricity, sound and light. The strength of his case was that while such constants had an increasing commercial significance for both academic research and commerce, the growth of traffic and especially of electrical traction in British cities made it increasingly difficult to undertake such sensitive investigation at existing institutions. Lodge argued that there should be two other main functions of a national laboratory: the maintenance of measurement standards and the conducting of long-term experimental research on materials, such as secular variation in elasticity and the influence of long exposure to light and heat.

While Lodge's account emphasised the academic rather than the commercial merits of the proposed institution, Lockyer, in his role as editor of *Nature*, emphasised the needs of industry in a contemporary leading article entitled "A Laboratory for Physical and Chemical Research". The article melodramatically bemoaned the alleged chaos and disorganisation of Britain's scientific system and the many industries that were supposedly languishing from a lack of scientific expertise. Although the journal conceded that the recent establishment of the Davy-Faraday Laboratory at the Royal Institution met some existing industrial needs, it argued that much more was needed. As a result of the various calls for an investigation of the subject, the British Association created a small committee "to consider the establishment of a national physical laboratory for the more accurate determination of physical constants, and other quantitative research".[5] The committee members were, however, not optimistic. Lord Rayleigh was not convinced that the time was ripe for such a move, and Richard Glazebrook later recalled that the committee felt it was hopeless to approach the government. In such an atmosphere, the committee achieved little and lapsed without taking further action.

Sir Douglas Galton and Lord Rayleigh's Committee

In his presidential address to the British Association in 1895, Sir Douglas Galton returned to the subject, and uttered a plea for the foundation of a national physical laboratory to be supported by government funding. Galton pointed out that there were already several government departments that carried out research for their own purposes. These departments included the Admiralty, which maintained the Greenwich Observatory and the Hydrographical Department. The War Office, too, had certain scientific departments, and the Treasury had an analytical laboratory. Other places that received indirect government support were the Ordnance and Geological Surveys, the Royal Mint, the Natural History Museum, Kew Gardens and the Standards Department of the Board of Trade at Westminster. Although British science had, in the past, progressed largely by means of voluntary support, Galton warned that continuing

to rely on voluntarism could have serious consequences for the future of British science. He concluded that the PTR in Berlin provided the appropriate model. The most advantageous situation would be for the government to allot a substantial sum of money to the extension of the Kew Observatory, in order to develop it along the lines of the Reichsanstalt. The new laboratory should be managed by the Royal Society. Kew Observatory was an obvious choice since, before the Royal Society had taken over its operations from the British Association in 1872, it had long been the national centre for calibrating magnetic and meteorological instruments.

Galton then drew up a memorandum that solicited the support of the British physics community. Almost every senior British physicist endorsed his view that:

> *if England is to keep pace with other countries in scientific progress, it is essential that such an institution be provided; and this can scarcely be maintained continuously on an adequate scale, except as a national laboratory supported mainly by the Government.*

The Prime Minister, Lord Salisbury, agreed on the importance of the proposed laboratory but thought that financing it would be particularly difficult. In his view, the government could only provide financial assistance for routine standardisation work, not fundamental research.

Despite Salisbury's reticence, wider support for a research-centred scheme was being successfully canvassed by Lord Rayleigh, whose brother-in-law, Arthur Balfour, was First Lord of the Treasury and an enthusiastic proponent of the laboratory. Rayleigh was thus able to use his influence to win more sympathy for the proposed institution, and in 1897, he set up an investigative committee headed by Lord Lister. This committee visited the Reichsanstalt and the other related German institutions, as well as the Board of Trade Standards Department and the Electrical Standards Laboratory at Whitehall, whose work foreshadowed that of the proposed laboratory. The committee found sufficient evidence to argue that British (or, more specifically, English) institutions had less adequate resources than their German counterparts. Accordingly, it resolved that a public institution should be established to determine and verify instruments, test materials, determine physical constants and undertake investigations into the strength and durability of metals.

Rayleigh's committee recommended that while the Royal Society should take nominal charge of the laboratory, its governing body should not be confined to fellows of the Royal Society but consist of an Executive Committee and General Board on which commercial interests should be represented. Following these recommendations, the first Executive Committee was appointed and Rayleigh was made chairman at the meeting of the council of the Royal Society on May 4th 1899. The General Board was comprised of seven *ex-officio* members, 24 direct nominees

of the Royal Society and 12 representatives of various technical societies. *Kew Observatory.*

There were several major matters still to be resolved by this new body when it first met, such as the extent to which the long-term annual financing of the Laboratory would be met, either by the government or commercial work, and, correlatively, the balance of different activities within the Laboratory's remit: metrology, commercial calibration, innovative research and technological development. However, the most immediate matter to be faced was the location of the new laboratory. Rayleigh's committee had followed Galton in proposing that the nucleus for the new institution should be Kew Observatory. And yet, as we shall see in the next chapter, a final decision about the location of the National Physical Laboratory was not taken until more than a year after its Executive Committee was first formed.

CHAPTER 2

The Establishment of the National Physical Laboratory

I believe that in the National Physical Laboratory we have the first instance of the State taking part in scientific research. The object of the scheme is, I understand, to bring scientific knowledge to bear practically upon our everyday industrial and commercial life, to break down the barrier between theory and practice, to effect a union between science and commerce. This afternoon's [opening] ceremony is not merely a meeting of the representatives of an ancient world-renowned scientific society for the purpose of taking over a new theatre of investigation and research. Is it not more than this? Does it not show in a very practical way that the nation is beginning to recognise that if its commercial supremacy is to be maintained, greater facilities must be given for furthering the application of science to commerce and industry?

The Prince of Wales, opening address of the NPL, March 19th 1902.

When the Executive Committee of the NPL began to consider where the laboratory should be located, Galton suggested (in his presidential address for the British Association in 1895) that the Kew Observatory be gradually extended into an institution similar to the Reichsanstalt. He then added that this would only be possible if the government accepted the extension of Kew and also aided the scheme with a grant of money.

Kew Observatory had been in existence since the end of the eighteenth century. Before the transit of Venus occurred in 1769 (when Venus passed across the disc of the sun), it became apparent that there were no facilities available for rigorous astronomical observation in Britain. Consequently, George III, who was a passionate amateur astronomer, gave orders for an observatory to be built in Old Deer Park in Richmond. The Observatory did not have an easy beginning, due to insufficient funds. When the British Association took control of Kew

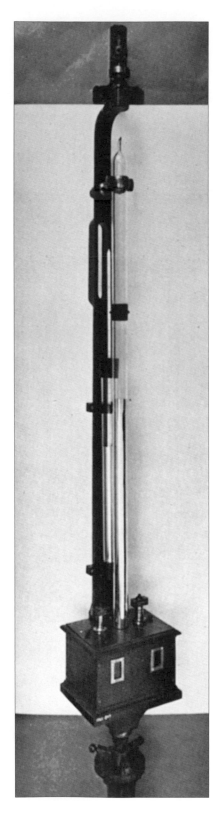

in 1842, its aim was to establish a centre for instrument testing and standardisation – especially those instruments concerned with meteorology and geomagnetism. Standard charges were made to cover the cost of the work. About 30 years later, the Royal Society took over the responsibility of the Kew Observatory and facilities, following a gift of £10,000 from John Peter Gassiot, a wealthy wine merchant and fellow of the Royal Society who was a great champion and benefactor of science. With the Royal Society in charge, the test work grew rapidly and soon a very large range of instruments was sent to Kew for verification.[6] When Galton advanced the claims for Kew in 1895, he felt that it could provide the nucleus for a larger institution, but that it would require a great deal of effort and money before it could operate on the same lines as the Reichsanstalt.

The committee for a national laboratory

Following Galton's suggestion, the British Association Committee on a National Laboratory began to work on a report on "The Establishment of a national physical laboratory for the more accurate Determination of Physical Constants and for other Quantitative Research".[7] Galton claimed that if Britain was to retain her industrial supremacy then there must be accurate standards for comparison available to research students and manufacturers: hence the emphasis on standardisation. The committee thought that there were certain types of research that lay outside the range of effort possible to one individual or to the universities, and these included: the observation of natural phenomena over a long period of time; the testing and verification of instruments for physical research; and the systematic accurate determination of physical constants of numerical data. The members of the committee argued that all of this work was of use for both science and industry. Their report led to the Treasury's decision to provide support.

The Treasury report

By the summer of 1897, the Treasury stated that another committee should be appointed to consider and report upon the desirability of establishing a national physical laboratory for the testing and verification of instruments for physical observation. The Treasury also wanted to know if the laboratory could construct and preserve standards of measurement, and determine physical constants and numerical data useful for scientific and industrial purposes. A committee was set up at once. A number of physicists (including Galton, Rayleigh, Glazebrook, Lodge and Kelvin) agreed that there was a growing need to undertake research into the basic physical constants to prevent the retardation of scientific progress. While the physicists on the committee thought that the proposed institution should undertake routine work, the representatives of the engineering industries disagreed. The engineers thought that some basic research was essential if the laboratory was to be of real assistance to industry. When the appointed

Treasury Committee report was published in 1897, it recommended that a national physical laboratory be founded. It also agreed that the proposed institution should be established at the national expense on similar lines to the Reichsanstalt, with a view to future extension.

The Treasury outlined the pecuniary assistance to be expected from public funds: this amounted to £4,000 per annum for five years. The Royal Society replied that the money would not be sufficient for a new institution, but might be adequate for a simple extension of Kew Observatory. By January 1899, a draft scheme for a national physical laboratory was officially submitted to the Treasury. Two months later it was approved.

The first meeting of the National Physical Laboratory

The first National Physical Laboratory (NPL) Executive Committee meeting was held on May 16th 1899 with Lord Rayleigh in the chair. Members of the General Board of the NPL were named and these consisted of spokesmen from the great technical societies representing the interests of several different sectors of industry including: the Institution of Civil Engineers, the Institution of Mechanical Engineers, the Institution of Electrical Engineers, the Institution of Naval Architects, the Iron and Steel Institute and the Society of Chemical Industry. By the second meeting on July 5th, it was recommended by the Royal Society (and by Rayleigh in particular) that Richard Tetley Glazebrook, FRS be appointed director of the Laboratory from January 1st 1900. Glazebrook had already established himself as someone with much business agility when he became senior bursar of Trinity College, Cambridge in 1895. As director of the NPL, he was able to combine his scientific knowledge and ability with business sagacity, sound judgement of mind and general mental vigour. He was regarded as a kindly man and held in an affectionate regard by many of his friends.

It was then suggested that a sub-committee of eminent scientists be appointed to prepare reports on the requirements of the following branches of laboratory work: Richard Strachey for meteorology, Arthur Rücker for terrestrial magnetism, and George Carey Foster and William Ayrton for electricity. Other work to be undertaken included mechanical engineering, chemistry and alloys, and legal standards. Optics was added at a later meeting.

The search for the site of the new laboratory

In October an account was opened for the NPL at the West End branch of the Bank of England. The next step was to determine the most suitable location for building the laboratory. Richard Glazebrook and Sir Courtney Boyle (a member of the Executive Committee) had communicated with HM Commissioner of Woods and Forests about Crown land that might possibly serve as sites for the NPL. Boyle, Glazebrook, Rayleigh and Rücker visited Eltham in Kent, the site being a field in Coldharbour Farm, Mottingham Lane, about one mile from the railway station. They

Early Kew Standard Barometer, 1860.

Teddington in the early 1900s.
top *Clarence Hotel.*
bottom *Queens Road.*

decided that while Eltham was a possible site for the laboratory, "the distance from a town on an unpunctual train was a grave disadvantage". Another consideration was that the "east side of London gets less sun than the west side". So Eltham's easterly location made it even less desirable.

The committee also visited Oxshott, Surrey but this site was unfea-

A garden party at Bushy House on the occasion of the opening of the Electrotechnics building in 1906.

sible as there were no sewers and no supply of water, gas or electricity, nor any accommodation for the staff. A third site mentioned by the Woods and Forest Department was in Hainault Forest, Essex. The nearest railway station was three miles away, and since this site had all of the disadvantages of Oxshott, it was thought unnecessary to visit.

A decision was then made to approach HM Commissioner of Woods and Forests with a view to obtaining a plot of ground in Old Deer Park in Richmond on which to erect the new building of the laboratory. By the end of January 1900, the Commissioner of Woods and Forests wrote to the Royal Society and offered to let a plot of about 15 acres, situated in the north-east corner of Old Deer Park. The Committee unanimously resolved that the offer of the commissioner be accepted. At this time it was also agreed to erect at once a second magnetic house where delicate magnetic measurement had to be undertaken, and was estimated to cost £1000. The Treasury agreed to make the necessary provisions to the NPL.

Bushy Park

At the next board meeting, Rayleigh reported that the General Board would have been prepared to approve the site in Old Deer Park if the site at Bushy Park had not been proposed as an alternative. The Board decided it would approve whichever of these sites, on further investigation, appeared best to the Executive Committee. Glazebrook was not, however, particularly satisfied with the site in Old Deer Park. He wrote to Arthur Schuster, a Cambridge mathematical physicist, that the buildings at Kew were too small and would be unsuitable for further extensions. Doubts about the proposed extension at Kew had also

been raised previously by a correspondent in *The Times* who had pointed out that the area was prone to flooding, and remarked that: "We do not wish to see a national laboratory at one time standing in a park and a few hours later looking like an islet in a lake." Hints that Bushy House in Teddington might possibly be offered as a site alternative to Kew had reached Glazebrook at the end of July. When Glazebrook was in Switzerland some three weeks later he received a telegram from the Office of Woods and Forests asking him: "Will Bushy House do for a national physical laboratory? Reply at once."

Arguments against building at Kew continued unabated. The Treasury wrote to Sir Courtney Boyle on October 24th that the opposition, both local and general, that the Richmond site had aroused had to be reckoned with. In these circumstances, Queen Victoria, under advice, expressed her willingness to assign the freehold of Bushy House for the laboratory. Sir Francis Mowett from the Treasury then suggested the use of Bushy House with 30 acres of land and the Treasury would provide the extra £2000 for alterations.

top *William, Duke of Clarence, later William IV. (Private Collection, print from the National Portrait Gallery, London.)* **bottom** *Queen Adelaide. (Copyright The British Museum.)*

Bushy House

The first substantial building on the site of Bushy House was begun in 1663 by Edward Proger, on the instruction of Charles II. Proger held the sinecure of Ranger at Bushy Park, and the lodge he built became the home of subsequent Rangers, which was an important position when the court was at Hampton Court Palace. Charles Montagu, First Earl of Halifax, became the Ranger in 1708 and repaired and added to Bushy Park House. It was later occupied by William IV who became Ranger of Bushy Park, and in 1837 his widow, Queen Adelaide, received the sinecure. After her death in 1849, the house became the gift of Queen Victoria who offered it to the exiled members of the French Royal family who lived there from 1865 to 1896. The house then reverted to Queen Victoria who later transferred it to the Royal Society in exchange for the De Vesci house in Pall Mall.

The Executive Committee decided that Bushy House was preferable to Old Deer Park. However, it noted that the annual amount allowed by the Treasury would make it difficult for it to maintain and administer a national physical laboratory at Bushy Park. Shortly after this decision was made, Oliver Lodge summarised the following type of work which ought to be done at the NPL: pioneer work, verification work, systematic measurements and examination of the properties of substances under all conditions, the precise determination of physical constants, observational work, testing instruments, constructional work, and designing new and perfect instruments.

Lodge's argument also persuaded the Executive Committee that these investigations should be undertaken at the laboratory: determining the properties of alloys of iron (physical, chemical, magnetic and electrical) and the conduction of heat by building materials. Various instruments would also be tested and these included: steam-pressure gauges, indicators, gauges of length, pyrometers for use in trade, and other instruments not tested by the Board of Trade. It appeared to the Committee that these investigations could be best conducted in a top-lighted room with a specially designed roof.

By the end of 1900, the First Commissioner of Her Majesty's Works wrote to the President of the Royal Society that: "Her Majesty, the Queen, has granted to the Commissioner of Works, by her Grace and Favour, Bushy House and Grounds for the use of the National Physical Laboratory under the direction of the Royal Society". The Commissioner of Works repaired the whole of the structure externally. The full range of repairs involved mending broken glass in skylights and sash-cords. It was also responsible for maintaining all drains, sewers, and water and gas supplies, as well as electricity services outside the building. The Royal Society was responsible for maintaining the ornamental grounds in good condition. It was also to keep buildings in tenantable repair and keep all internal service pipes and fittings connected with the lighting and heating in proper working order.

After the building had been refitted and repaired, opportunities for work were opening in many directions. By then, the NPL had absorbed the standard and verification work of Kew Observatory; indeed, one of NPL's first departments was known as the Observatory Department. The thermometry investigations (which included gas and electric thermometers) at Kew were being continued by Dr Harker, assistant in the Physics Department. The Laboratory began testing gun-sights following an enquiry from the Director of Naval Contracts. Glazebrook received permission to serve on the optical standards committee of the Optical Society, and on a War Office committee set up to secure a standard uniformity in screws used in the manufacture of the breech mechanisms of guns.

top *Board Of Trade current balance.* **bottom** *Board of Trade standard ohm.*

To help create a feeling of institutional camaraderie, the Finance Committee of the NPL recommended, in early May 1901, that the director, Richard Glazebrook, and his family should occupy as their private residence, the second floor of the main block of the north wing of Bushy House together with three sitting rooms on the first floor of the main block facing south and west. Glazebrook's residence also included a

The National Physical Laboratory.

*The President of the Royal Society and Lord Rayleigh,
Chairman of the General Board of the Laboratory,
request the honour of the Company of*

and a Lady

*on the occasion of the Opening of the Laboratory,
at Bushy House, Teddington, by
His Royal Highness The Prince of Wales,
at 4 p.m. on Wednesday, March 19th 1902.*

*Special train from
Waterloo.*

*The favour of an answer addressed to the Director,
The National Physical Laboratory, Bushy House, Teddington,
is requested. On receipt of this, tickets of admission to the
ceremony will be sent.*

top *Official opening of the
National Physical Laboratory by
HRH the Prince of Wales, March
19th 1902.* **above** *Invitation to the
opening of the laboratory.*
opposite *Agenda for the opening.*

wine cellar, a coal cellar and a bicycle shed with a small enclosed yard – accommodation not unlike that of an Oxbridge college and conferring on its inhabitant similar status to the head of a college.

As the scheme for converting the ground floor and basement of Bushy House into a physics laboratory got under way, the consequences of separating financial provisions from administrative control were of secondary concern. The Executive Committee began to consider the possibility of finding industrial support for the new venture and of securing an increase in the government's contribution. It was soon clear that the laboratory in Bushy Park required capital expenditure to avoid a delay in the testing programme. Moreover, capital costs greatly exceeded the original estimates by £5,000. The Treasury warned the Royal Society on a number of occasions that their figures must be considered final. The delay in starting work, due to the transfer of site and increase in expenditure, caused the Treasury to view the new laboratory with suspicion. With the capital expenditure reaching £17,000, the entire scheme proved to be considerably more expensive than expected. It was fortunate for the NPL that it was

THE NATIONAL PHYSICAL LABORATORY.

AGENDA

Wednesday March 19th 1902

Sir William Huggins P.R.S.   in the Chair.

The President calls on
Lord Rayleigh
to address the meeting.

The President calls on
The Rt. Honble G. W. Balfour M.P.
President of the Board of Trade.
to address the meeting.

His Royal Highness the Prince of Wales
declares the Laboratory open.

The President calls on
1. The Lord Chancellor
2. Lord Kelvin.
3. The Lord Mayor.
to propose, second, and support a vote of thanks
to His Royal Highness.
The President conveys the thanks of the Meeting to His Royal Highness.

The Company adjourn to Bushy House to inspect the Laboratory.

able to enlist the support of the new Prince of Wales in early 1902 through Rayleigh's influence. The future monarch not only gave his unqualified support to the project, but he also spoke of the important work being done for both science and commerce. With royal approval of the broader aspects of industrial research, the Executive Committee could pursue more open-ended and innovative research than it might otherwise have done.

CHAPTER 3

Building the National Physical Laboratory

I n 1901, work began on converting the ground floor and basement of Bushy House into a physics laboratory. Other parts of the building were arranged as temporary laboratories for electrical, magnetic and thermometric work, in addition to metallurgical and chemical research, which were all considered to be the most fundamental areas that had to be accommodated first. By April, the contract for the engineering building had been settled on satisfactory terms and the building had begun. Inside Bushy House, men were at work on the heating apparatus and the gas and water supplies.

Kew Magnetic Observatory

Sometime towards the end of 1900, a proposal had been made by the London United Tramway Company to electrify its lines in the district close to the Kew Magnetic Observatory. A clause for the protection of government observatories had previously been inserted in acts relating to electrical traction. In April 1901, the Treasury had asked the Royal Society whether it would approve the removal of the Magnetic Observatory at Old Deer Park, Richmond, to some other suitable site. A Magnetic Observatory committee appointed by the Executive Committee of the NPL came to the conclusion that the new observatory should be free from disturbances due to electrical traction, and it was decided that it should be at least ten miles from any electric railway or tram line.

Glazebrook, in his search for a suitable location for the Magnetic Observatory, decided to visit some places during the summer of 1901 by bicycle. As he later recalled, access was difficult, horse hire was expensive and motor cars were available only for the most affluent.

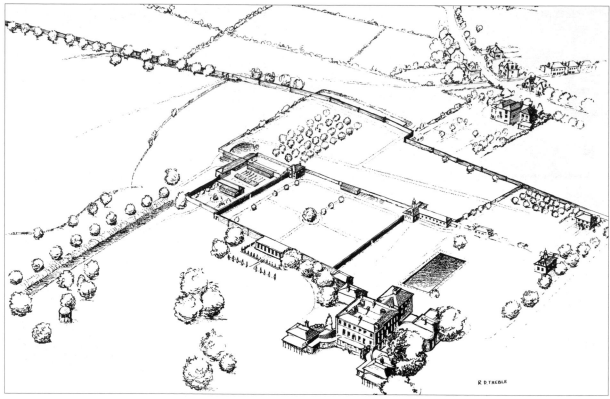

Drawing of the NPL site in 1900 by R D Treble.

So, with his bicycle he spent an interesting time in many out-of-the way parts of England and Scotland. The Executive Committee made an exhaustive report on the question of location, and chose a number of sites in such places as Exmoor in Devonshire, Farnham in Dorset, Eskdale in Dumfriesshire, and the Cheviot District in the Lammermuir Hills in Berwickshire. It recommended Eskdale as the most suitable location. The cost of removal and rebuilding was in part met by the tramway company. The observatory was erected there and worked as a branch of the NPL until its transfer to the Meteorological Office some years later.

The work undertaken at the Kew Magnetic Observatory included: registration of magnetic elements and measurements of the curves; observation of earth currents; observation of atmospheric electricity; and seismological observations. Magnetic elements were important to geophysicists who developed theories about how magnetic fields changed over time which, in turn, affected navigation. The determination of earth currents was important to telegraphy and telephony, while seismological observations were needed for the colonies where volcanoes posed real threats. Certain kinds of work were still carried out at Kew such as testing of ships' compasses and of recording instruments.

The headquarters of the superintendent of magnetic work were to be at Kew or Bushy House, where he would supervise the magnetic

experimental work. The staff at the new observatory in Eskdalemuir consisted of two trained observers and a boy. Additionally, two buildings and various rooms were required. They built two Magnetic Houses, one for absolute measures and another for experimental work. There were three underground rooms: one for recording instruments, the second for eye-reading variometers and experimental work, and the third for seismographic work. They also set up a photographic room and a room for earth-current apparatus.

In June, work on the Engineering Department was being carried out. The laboratory of this department was 80 feet by 50 feet with a drawing office, engine and boiler houses, and an attached storage battery room. A 60 kilowatt Parsons' turbine and dynamo were fitted for the supply of power. The engineering superintendent, Dr Thomas Stanton, was responsible for the care and proper supervision of the machines including the steam-heating apparatus of the main laboratory.

Staff recruitment

The staff of the departments were divided into two sections: one for the construction of standards, the carrying out of tests and the issue of certificates; and the other for research. Several months later, a staff committee was appointed to consider the question of the staff and the laboratory, and to make arrangements for the salaries and terms of appointment. Much of the work undertaken by the staff involved large

top *Parsons' Turbine, 1902.*
bottom *Thomas E Stanton, Superintendent of the Engineering Department.*

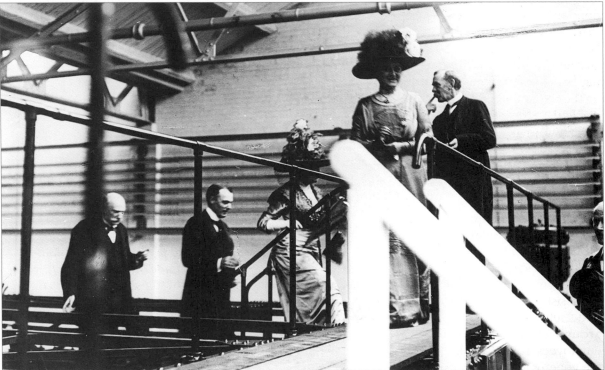

Tank under construction, 1910.

amounts of routine work for rather small salaries. Due to employment opportunities for physicists being so scarce at the time, it was possible to recruit staff of excellent qualifications for a scientific institution that had as yet no reputation. Nevertheless, the existing reputations of Glazebrook and Stanton attracted interest in NPL work from the most highly qualified scientists of the time.

The NPL thus experienced no difficulty in finding suitable employees and as the NPL grew so did the number of its staff. The profile of new recruits was remarkably uniform: most were expected to possess first-class honours degrees, they were in their twenties and had been trained as physicists (usually at one of the new university colleges or at Owens College in Manchester, which had been founded in 1851). It was these graduates, of a high scientific calibre, who helped to establish the repu-tation of the NPL in the eyes of the scientific community and industry. Moreover, since the employment opportunities for physicists remained bleak until after the First World War, there was never any difficulty in finding replacements for them.

As engineering superintendent, Stanton received £400 per annum, the assistant in the Department of Physics was paid between £200 and £300 per annum, and the junior assistants' salaries averaged around £100 per annum. The low salaries offered to the NPL employees from 1900 till 1919 may have reflected the reluctance of the government to grant the desired financial support. Or perhaps

top *Opening of the William Froude National Tank, July 5th 1911 showing Admiral Capps, USN, Marchioness of Bristol and Sir Alfred Yarrow.* **bottom** *Lord Rayleigh, Marquis and Marchioness of Bristol and Sir Richard Glazebrook.*

Staff of Kew Observatory Department 1906.

top *Barometer testing.*
bottom *Checking the accuracy of sextants.*

the government knew that posts could be filled easily. Either way, the Royal Society and the Treasury were often in conflict about the finances of the NPL, with the Royal Society wanting more money and the Treasury saying "no".

The William Froude National Tank

In October 1900, the naval architect and draughtsman in the Royal Dockyard, Sir Nathaniel Barnaby, wrote to Glazebrook and enquired whether the Laboratory would consider the establishment of a tank for testing ship models. At the end of December, Glazebrook reported that the committee for the Institution of Naval Architects generally approved the site at Bushy Park for the installation of a naval tank for experimental purposes. It was agreed by the NPL that a sum of £15,000 would suffice to build and equip a tank. However, at the beginning of 1901, it was considered impossible to raise the funds required. Another seven years would pass before Barnaby wrote again to the NPL to inform them that Alfred Yarrow, a marine engineer and shipbuilder, had promised to provide the Council of the Institution of Naval Architects the sum of £20,000 for the erection and equipment of the tank. The offer was accepted and by early 1910 the William Froude National Tank, as it became known, was built. The Admiralty owned a tank at Haslar that had become well known through the work of the engineer and naval architect, William Froude. By the end of the year, the tank was operational.

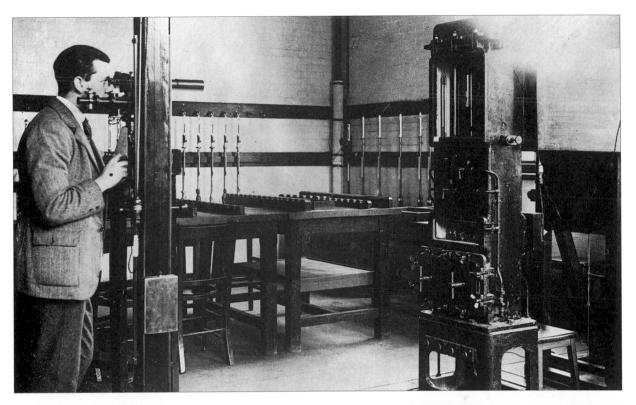

The transference of Kew Observatory

At the end of 1900 the Meteorological Committee at Kew informed Glazebrook that it would not be able to continue its subsidy of £400 per annum. This caused much concern to the Executive Committee: after all, Kew had been in the forefront of advances in meteorology and kindred sciences for more than half a century. The potential discontinuation of the Kew grant would have also involved the loss of international prestige associated with the name, Kew. In January 1910, the Treasury thought that the meteorological work at Kew should be transferred to Teddington. This transfer of work meant that Teddington would have to provide buildings to house the work and also to provide additional accommodation for administration.

A month later, Joseph Larmor, the president of the Royal Society, wrote to inform the Treasury that the Royal Society was prepared to carry through, as a temporary arrangement, a proposal whereby the working of Kew Observatory should be divided between the NPL and the Meteorological Committee of the Royal Society. Larmor added that the work would need an expenditure of £550 per annum (£200 would be contributed from the funds of the NPL and the remaining £300 would have to come from the Treasury). The testing of thermometers, telescopes and certain other optical instruments long associated with Kew had remained there, as well as a considerable amount of meteorological and magnetic work.

Most of the NPL's early work dealt with routine fee-paying work such as the testing of thermometers, the standardisation and calibration of scientific instruments sent in for testing, and various physical and chemical analyses. In the beginning, the number of tests the NPL undertook was much smaller than had been anticipated. Glazebrook claimed he knew why this disparity occurred: "Englishmen are conservative: the high-class maker does not want tests, he knows his products are good; his cheap and nasty rival does not want the tests, they will expose his weaknesses." (During this period, "English" is quite synonymous with "British": the use of the word "national" meant English in practice, but British in legal terms.)

Nature protested that while the Laboratory's principal aim was: "the application of science to industry, it should be prepared to lead the way in exploring new fields which are possibly and quite probably not immediately remunerative." It also warned of the future dangers associated with limiting the amount of research. The almost catastrophic results of postponing urgently needed research on optical glass at the start of the First World War meant that the scientists at the NPL thought that the Treasury should have provided extra funding.

Early work

During the winter of 1901-1902, the alterations at Bushy House were completed at a total cost of £19,000 (£5,000 more than the original estimate of £14,000). Compared to similar institutions in Germany and

Thermometer testing in Bushy House pre-1918.

the United States, the NPL's cost was small. The cost of the Reichsanstalt (which opened in 1887) was £200,000, and the Versuchsanstalt in Berlin cost £137,000. At the National Bureau of Standards in Washington DC, £115,000 had been spent on buildings and equipment with an annual grant of £19,000.

By early 1902, test work had only just begun at the NPL and the income from fees was less than expected. The Treasury believed that the Laboratory should, and could, become self-supporting; moreover, the Treasury also believed that eventually there would be no need for its financial support. Throughout 1902, there was a rapid increase in routine test work. At the end of 1899, when testing was still done at Kew, 225,532 instruments were verified, of which clinical thermometers accounted for 16,020. During 1902, the NPL had verified 311,025 instruments, of which 22,856 were clinical thermometers. In December, Glazebrook reported that arrangements had been made, in consultation with the India Office, for the installation of the apparatus for predicting the Indian tides. The Laboratory authorities undertook the future calculations of the tide tables.

Treasury stipends

By 1903, the work of the Laboratory had begun to gather momentum. Despite the increased income resulting from test work, the overall financial position of the Laboratory continued to cause the Executive Committee grave anxiety because expenditures were exceeding income. When the inconvenience of a rapid turnover of staff had become apparent, the Executive Committee warned the Treasury that the stipends paid were not commensurate with the work: the low pay was insufficient to retain the service of men of calibre for any length of time.

The Treasury advised the council of the Royal Society to formulate some "constructive proposals" concerning the future of the NPL. Reluctantly, the Executive Committee recognised that it would have to accept the Treasury grant of £4,000 for 1904-05 while evidence was being prepared. In its report, the committee pointed out to the Treasury that the annual grant for the Reichsanstalt was £16,000, for the Versuchsanstalt £15,000 and for the National Bureau of Standards £19,000. The NPL had made it clear that some future expansion was not only desirable but also essential, if it was to carry out the tasks for which it had been established.

Buildings of the laboratory

The Executive Committee estimated that the Laboratory's original capital grant of £19,000 would need to be supplemented by a further £28,750 for new buildings and apparatus. The annual grant would need to be increased to £6,000 over the following four years to allow the salaries of the scientific staff to be raised. The estimated capital expenditure was to be used for the Engineering Department (£14,200), an electrotechnics building (£7,500), a metrology building (£5,500), an optics building (£500) and a chemistry laboratory (£1,000).

The Electrotechnics Laboratory was to be well equipped for the ordinary measurement of electrical resistance, capacity and inductance. There was a considerable demand from electrical suppliers and manufacturers for testing of ammeters, wattmeters and voltmeters for powerful alternating currents. To accommodate all of this work, a building with an area of about 100 feet by 75 feet was needed. The demand for tests of measures of length, gauges and screws increased steadily and accommodation in the Metrology Department was inadequate. Though tests on optical instruments had long been in the Observatory Department, it needed to extend and improve work in this area. The German export of scientific apparatus and optical glasses trebled in the ten years from 1888-1898: its competitive edge in industry was facilitated by its annual value of about £75,000. The Chemistry Laboratory was too small for the work to be done; it was practically impossible to carry out analytical tests. With these requirements in mind, the Executive Committee asked the Treasury for £28,750. A reply from the Treasury came rapidly. This response supported the view at the NPL that the speed of a Treasury reply was inversely proportional to the amount of good news it contained.

The Treasury thought the amount of money requested was far too large, and it was suggested that the Executive Committee reconsider which of the new works and items were most pressing and cut plans accordingly. Not surprisingly, the reaction of the Executive Committee and of the Royal Society was that of disappointment. This time, the Executive Committee replied more forcefully. It speculated that if the Laboratory remained under-developed, this would limit the powers and opportunities for Britain. The Royal Society remarked that, "if the nation's industries could not be served by the National Physical Laboratory, then the Treasury should consider whether the Royal Society would be justified in continuing its present responsibility."

The NPL's Executive Committee also informed the Treasury that it was planning an audience with the Prime Minister to seek further government aid. Rayleigh arranged a meeting with his brother-in-law, the Prime Minister, Arthur Balfour, accompanied by Austen Chamberlain and the president of the Board of Trade in the autumn of 1904. The meeting had the desired effect: the Treasury agreed to the request for £28,750 with an additional £5,000 for 1905-06. The Treasury also hoped that the NPL would receive an annual £5,000 for the next four or five years. The Executive Committee regarded this as a promising start.

On February 19th 1905, the Executive Committee decided there was a need for additional buildings to house the increased amount of work of calibrations for industry. It did not expect to be doing fee-paying work for a long time: in the early years, it was uncertain how much of this work it would be required to undertake, and it was not clear if the financial assistance needed to build the new buildings would be forth-coming. With this uncertainty, the NPL decided not to embark on new research programmes, and instead placed emphasis upon fee-paying work which did not depend upon new equipment and facilities. When the Treasury finally came through with the much-needed money, the NPL was able to begin its expansions.

CHAPTER 4

New Departments and Buildings

At the beginning of 1905, Robert Chalmer of the Treasury Department informed the NPL that the Treasury had asked parliament to vote for an additional grant of £1,500 so that the NPL would have £5,000 for 1905-6. The Executive Committee also stipulated that no member of the staff below the director and superintendent of the Engineering Department should receive a higher salary than £400 per annum. It appeared to the committee that it might be essential in the near future to appoint a superintendent in the Physics Department and that it should be able to offer him more than £400 per annum. The committee was also bound to point out once again that a total sum of £6,000 per year was very much less than the grants to corresponding institutions in Germany and America.

The Building Committee

In the following month, plans were made to erect an electrotechnics building as well as a building for metrology. The Engineering Department

top *Electrotechnics Building, 1906.* bottom *Large bay in the Electrotechnics Building.*

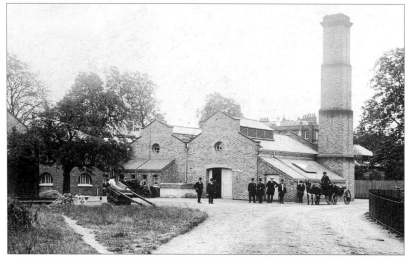

top *General view of one of the instrument testing stations in the Electrotechnics Building.*
bottom *Engineering Building and Power House, 1902-03.*

The opening of the Electrotechnics Building, 1906, was front page news.

needed a 300-ton testing machine costing £7,000; the building to house it cost £5,000. The money available for buildings and equipment came from the £5,000 Treasury grant for 1905-6 and an anonymous donation of £2,000. During the late spring, the Building Committee had agreed to enter a contract with Messrs. Mowlem for the erection of the proposed electrotechnical building at a cost of £5,641. Around the same time, Rayleigh recommended that Glazebrook's stipend be raised to £1,300 and that an allowance of £25 be made towards the cost of maintaining the gardens.

The chemical industry and commercial testing

During early 1905, there was a marked increase in the number of chemical tests undertaken. Sir William Ramsay, then vice-president of the Institute of Chemistry of Great Britain and Ireland, wrote to Glazebrook about the commercial testing of chemical material. With all of the test work the NPL undertook in return for fees, Ramsay thought the NPL had crossed the boundary into commercial work. Rayleigh began to receive letters from both the Institute of Chemistry and the Society of Public Analysts expressing the fear that the NPL was being used for commercial chemical analyses. The Executive Committee initially dismissed these fears as groundless and claimed that they had not diverged from standard practice.

Ramsay urged that an honourable understanding should be made that the NPL should confine itself to purely public work and that commercial testing of all kinds should be refused. The matter had been brought to parliament. Reginald McKenna, Chancellor of the Exchequer, explained that except for government work and for some few special cases that came individually before the committee, chemical analyses were only undertaken by the NPL when required to elucidate some physical or mechanical question under investigation.

Lord Rayleigh remarked that the Executive Committee had no desire

The Daily Mirror

THE MORNING JOURNAL WITH THE SECOND LARGEST NET SALE.

No. 828. | Registered at the G. P. O. as a Newspaper. | WEDNESDAY, JUNE 27, 1906. | One Halfpenny.

THE SECRETARY FOR WAR OPENS AN ELECTRICAL LABORATORY.

There was a remarkable gathering of scientists at the National Physical Laboratory at Teddington on Monday, when Mr. Haldane, the Secretary for War, opened the electrical building. The photograph shows Mr. Haldane speaking. On his left sits Lord Rayleigh. *(Daily Mirror* photograph.)

Lord Rayleigh, president of the laboratory, speaking at the opening of the electrical building at Teddington. Mr. Haldane said that he was present not merely as an individual, for the Government were keenly interested in the development of s... *(Daily Mirror* photograph.)

45

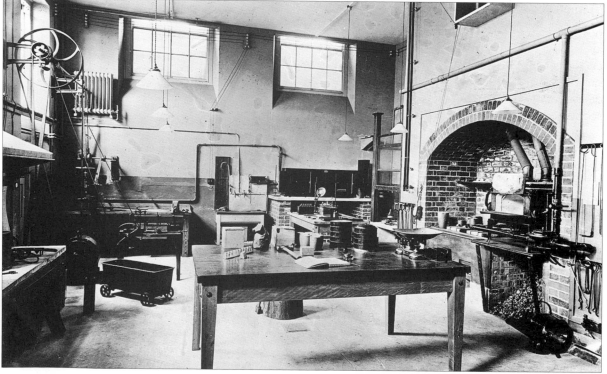

The Rt. Hon. R B Haldane speaking at the opening of the Electrotechnics Building, 1906.

to depart from the practice as stated in the Test Pamphlet of 1903: it did not wish to interfere with the work of professional chemists and did not believe that such interference took place in the Laboratory. Rayleigh also pointed out, however, that chemical work would be required in certain branches of government work. Moreover, if a test on material, ordinarily physical or mechanical in its nature, required a chemical determination for its completion, such determination came within the scope of the Laboratory's work.

The committee also stated that it endeavoured to make the NPL of service to English industry in a manner similar to that in which the German industry had been helped by its two great institutions in Berlin. It also restated the role of the NPL as a public institution which was established for standardising and verifying instruments, for testing material and for the determination of physical constants. Eventually Rayleigh agreed to amend the Laboratory's test pamphlets to make it quite clear that chemical testing was only carried out in conjunction with physical testing, and then only when strictly necessary.

New buildings and new work

Despite the protracted debate about commercial testing, a considerable amount of work was done during 1905-6 and throughout 1907. By the end of 1907, the NPL had erected buildings for engineering, electricity, metallurgical chemistry and metrology, and the Treasury had increased

top *Electricity Laboratory in Bushy House, 1906.* **bottom** *The First Metallurgical Laboratory in the old kitchen in Bushy House, 1906.*

47

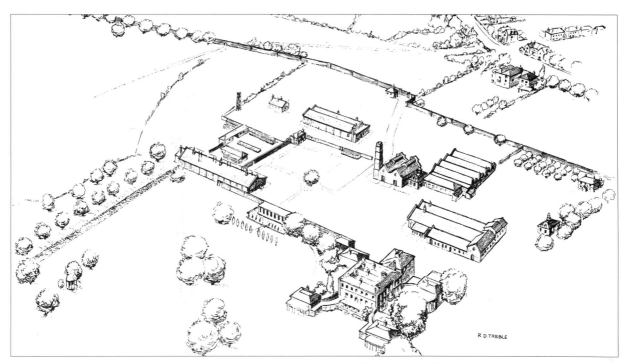

NPL site in 1910 by R D Treble.

its annual £5,000 grant to £10,000. In the same period, Sir John Brunner made a donation of £5,000 towards equipment for the Electrotechnical Building. With the growth of these buildings, the annual expenditure increased, since lighting, heating, attendance, cleaning and other maintenance charges had to be met.

During its first seven years, the NPL had undergone many changes including building new laboratories and a major reorganisation of the departments. Requests for test work increased as well. By the beginning of 1908, various letters were received requesting tests on wire rope, magnetic tests on steel rails with a chemical analysis and an examination into causes of fracture of steel shafts. The National Bureau of Standards in Washington DC enquired about the international unit of candle power and also asked about tests on instruments for radiotelegraphy. Christchurch Observatory in New Zealand had asked for a loan of a magnetometer for its Antarctic expedition. The Laboratory was now ready to begin a new phase in its development. Despite the continued growth and development in the Laboratory and increased demands for tests, the period from 1908 until the beginning of the First World War in 1914 continued to be one of struggle between the Royal Society and the Treasury.

Aeronautical research

The Executive Committee had also extended its research programmes to include a study of problems of travel by air as well as by sea. A tank was installed to enable shipping research to be carried out. Plans were drawn up for a comprehensive programme for aeronautical research.

Testing transformer, 1907.

A division was set up to deal with problems associated with experimental road tracks and testing of road materials. This was one of the few times before the First World War that the Laboratory took on a pioneer role in a new scientific endeavour. A substantial commitment to aeronautical research lasted till 1970, when the work was transferred to RAE Farnborough. The industrial aerodynamics work (looking at the effect of wind round buildings, smoke stacks, bridges, etc.) remained with the NPL for a few more years, but was then transferred to the National Maritime Institute (later privatised to become British Maritime Technology).

Three of the earliest electric furnaces made at the NPL about 1910-12.

As Russell Moseley has remarked, the speed at which the aeronautical work was carried out during the First World War, and the manner in which funds were made available, illustrated clearly the government's ambivalent attitude towards research at this time.[8] Many of the scientists at the NPL felt that much of the research undertaken for industry by the NPL was not as well-funded as it should be; they felt they should receive as much money as scientists who were paid by industry. In contrast, aeronautical research promised military benefits and was, therefore, looked upon very favourably. While the Royal Society struggled to obtain funds for the Laboratory's standards work and general research programme, money for aeronautical investigations was given freely. For example, in the financial year 1914-15, the annual and capital grants for aeronautical work was £12,550, whereas the grants-in-aid for the rest of the work in the Laboratory amounted to only £7,000.

Support from the industrialists

Although the Treasury provided ample money from the start for aeronautical research, the amount of work this research created in other areas of the Laboratory was substantial, particularly in the Engineering and Metallurgy Departments. The need for additional buildings to absorb the increase in work due to the NPL's expansion could not be met by the annual grant from the Treasury. In May of 1909, the Executive Committee outlined a comprehensive buildings programme stressing the need for new metallurgy and administration buildings; it concluded that extensions to existing buildings would not suffice – new buildings would need to be erected if the Laboratory was to run effectively.

The report estimated that £30,000 would be needed. The Treasury's immediate reply indicated that it would not consider the possibility of

Two views of the road testing machine, 1911.

a capital grant for the year 1910-11. Glazebrook decided to enlist the support of some industrialists. A few days later, the industrialist Sir Julius Wernher wrote to Glazebrook offering £10,000 for the proposed metallurgy building. Meanwhile, Glazebrook's hopes that the Treasury would provide the essential funding were not realised. The Treasury would only promise a grant of £2,000 "for additional buildings" with no indication of further financial aid.

Glazebrook arranged a meeting with Sir George Murray, permanent secretary to the Treasury, and was able to get a verbal promise from the Treasury of a similar grant for the next two years. The Royal Society expressed its frustration that, "economy in construction at the National Physical Laboratory has been pushed as far as seems suitable to a national institution, and so far as to excite unfavourable comparisons between the mere engineering sheds at Bushy and the architectural buildings of similar institutions in other countries." Despite these remarks, the Treasury only gave the NPL the continuation of the £5,000 building grant over the next two years as Murray had promised. Moreover, the Treasury argued that this money was to be used on the understanding that the whole scheme would be completed with this assistance.

Although the campaign for funds from the Treasury was not very successful, private sources gave sufficient money so that work could begin on the new metallurgical and optical laboratories and the administration building, which were eventually housed in one building. The new buildings were eventually opened by Arthur Balfour, the former Prime Minster, in July 1913. Much of the frustration experienced by the NPL administration from 1899 to 1914, was attributed to the financial policy of the Treasury under successive governments, and a lack of scientific expertise within that department. Its civil servants seemed unable or unwilling to sympathise with the more fundamental work of the laboratory; moreover, they were convinced that scientific research should ultimately be financially self-supporting.

CHAPTER 5

Optical Glass

Optical glass had been in production in Britain since the 1850s and much of the theoretical work which made future developments possible had been undertaken by British scientists. Until 1880, Britain enjoyed marked advantages in the manufacture of optical glass, but by the final decades of the nineteenth century Germany began to take the lead thanks to government investment.

The German government awarded grants for research and also allocated grants for capital expenditure on new buildings and equipment; moreover, the German War Office had already begun to place large orders for optical instruments during peacetime. This combination of factors had an immediate beneficial effect on stimulating new developments in optical techniques. This state of affairs had not gone unnoticed by Sir Douglas Galton in 1897, when he gave evidence to Rayleigh's committee on the founding of a national laboratory. Galton had remarked that, "the Germans by their research have now got the market for all optical glass."

With the expanding market of Germany's optical glass industry, large investments were undertaken in research. It was not only the British who relied on the Jena Glass industries in Germany before the war, continental countries, especially France, had made even greater use of German optical glass. By 1912, the Jena Glass works was able to offer 90 standard varieties of glass whereas the British firm

Walter Rosenhain.

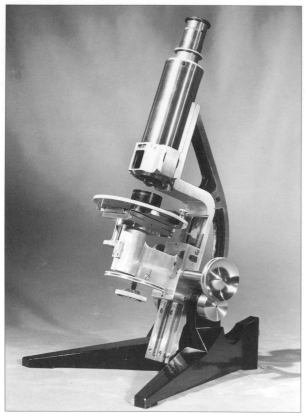

Rosenhain optical microscope.

of Chance Brothers could list only 20.

A former employee of Chance Brothers, Walter Rosenhain, joined the NPL in 1910 and was made superintendent of the Metallurgy Department. A few months after Rosenhain began working at the NPL, Glazebrook and Chance Brothers drew up a report concerning the state of optical glass production in Britain. While the firm assured Glazebrook that it hoped to produce some of the glasses required in co-operation with the NPL, it lacked sufficient funds. Glazebrook then obtained the support of the astronomer Sir David Gill in securing funds through the NPL's General Board. By March 1912, the Executive Committee devised a scheme of work suggested by Rosenhain. It discussed the matter with the War Office and the Admiralty and was promised private aid of somewhere between £300 and £800.

On October 12th 1912, a report was circulated to various government officials and industrial leaders about the pressing need for the manufacture of optical glass in Britain. The report emphasised the military value of glass and a rather prophetic note was made by one of the leading opticians that, "in the event of a war with Germany, which I trust will never occur, a shortage of optical glass would simply paralyse the optical trade." He went on to remark that while the army and navy depended on the manufacture of optical instruments, if a war broke out, the production would come to a standstill – probably with disastrous results. One factor which contributed to the postponement of optical glass research at the NPL was the financial necessity of routine work in return for fees.

The British Science Guild

One of the most influential of the organisations engaged in advancing the claims of science was the British Science Guild. The guild had been founded by Sir Norman Lockyer in 1905 to draw attention to the importance of science, and to undertake the task of "applying scientific method to public affairs". Taking advantage of the opportunity created by the outbreak of the First World War, the guild urged that public funds for the support of research be increased. Further weight was added to these demands by the Institute of Industry and Science – established in 1915 in response to the deficiencies revealed by the war, this organisation consisted of scientists and industrialists. It campaigned for a ministry of industry to deal with related problems of research and education for developing essential industries. The Royal Society also took on an important, albeit indirect, role in mobilising scientific opinion for the government. The council of the Royal Society was, however, unwilling to endorse any recommendation directly affecting the government or industry, and limited its committee to problems of a purely scientific nature.

NPL staff claimed that inadequate funding for scientific research and the lack of organised science in Britain had serious consequences during the First World War. When hostilities broke out in August 1914, scientists in Britain believed that Germany's well-funded and organised scientific research meant that it was well-prepared and had, by then, made it a leader in many industrial fields. Since the middle of the nineteenth century, Britain had relied on importing a wide range of manufactured goods from Germany, and many of these were now in short supply. Though Britain had supplies of dyestuffs, photographic developers, synthetic dyes, bronze powders, and filter papers as well as chemical and optical glassware from its colonies, there was now a shortage of these supplies in Britain. At the start of the war, scientists were arguing that Britain's industrial power had been undermined since the latter part of the nineteenth century and that Britain was not prepared to fight a modern scientific and technological war. Yet since relations between Britain and Germany were not generally hostile at the turn of the century, perhaps it was not obvious that Germany would be a likely enemy in any future European war.

The goods formerly imported from Germany were essential for manufacturing material upon which depended Britain's chance of military success. Dyestuffs were required for uniforms, acetone was needed for explosives, optical glass was used in the making of range-finders, magnetos were essential for transport and a whole range of chemicals were involved in the preparation of drugs. British manufacturers relied on Germany for more than 50 per cent of their imports of optical glass, and had not invested in research and technical developments in this area. Britain had, however, invested in other areas, including telegraphy, radio work, electrical manufacture and chemical production. At the start of the war, the government's administrative machinery for promoting research was limited. Research directly related to war effort became the responsibility of the War Office, the Admiralty and the Ministry of Munitions.

At an early stage in the conflict, there was much heated debate in

Rosenhain levelling device for optical metrology.

Britain about how Germany managed to use science so successfully for industrial purposes. Some suggested that its success was due to the intellectual achievements of brilliant scientists. But Britain, for its part, had not lacked creative and brilliant scientists. Instead Germany's success was linked to its organisation in the training of scientists, the organisation of research and the management of laboratories to apply the results of their research.

By 1914, a large number of applied scientists were working in German industry. In Britain industrial research was only just beginning to emerge. At the beginning of the twentieth century, there were 4,000 chemists employed in German industry of whom 84 per cent qualified at university, while in Britain there were 1,500 chemists employed in industry and only 34 per cent had similar qualifications. The situation had hardly changed by 1914; moreover, British chemists who worked in industry were poorly paid in comparison to industrial workers.

After the First World War began, the government decided to take a hand in actively promoting scientific research with a bearing on the problems and process of industry. A unique opportunity had thus arisen to correct existing deficiencies and to create new institutions. From the onset of the war, demands were made for the integration of science with the war effort. The novelist H G Wells complained in the summer of 1915 that, "on our side we have so far produced hardly any novelty at all, except in the field of recruiting posters."

Measures were taken to bring scientists into closer contact with the armed forces and the NPL hoped that this would foster a scientific spirit within industry as well as increase the number of trained scientists who would be required after the war. Not long after the war had begun, it was realised that the shortage of dyestuffs had placed the British textile trades in such a situation the "magnitude, gravity and imminence of which, pointed to the necessity of government action". In response to these fears, an investigative committee was appointed by the Board of Trade under Lord Haldane. It recommended that the government help fund a scheme for establishing a large dye manufacturing company. The company was known as British Dyes Limited and was to be financed by government subsidies and industrial contributions.

In December 1914, the universities branch of the Board of Education submitted a memorandum which argued that universities did not produce an adequate number of research workers. This situation probably arose because the research jobs did not pay well and were low in numbers, so students chose to go elsewhere. It was estimated that there were only 400 full-time students in universities in England and Wales doing research which had any relation to industry. In contrast, there were 3,046 students engaged in such research in German institutions and technical schools.

A central advisory committee was to be appointed by the president of the Board of Education to give support to various universities and technical colleges, but the progress of the war rendered the plan impractical. Subsequently, the Board of Education decided that so long as there was a war, it was going to be impossible to undertake long-term plans to extend scientific education. To meet the objectives of training scientists for the war effort, a committee was formed under Sir William McCormick (chairman of the Advisory Committee on Grants to Universities). The McCormick Committee recommended the creation of the Advisory Council for Scientific and Industrial Research in 1915, and in the following year the Department of Scientific and Industrial Research (DSIR) was established. The new department was responsible for promoting co-operative research in industry through the use of a fund of a million pounds provided by parliament. The money was to be used to co-ordinate scientific manpower requirements, for scientific research projects and for postgraduate training.

With the outbreak of the war, Britain had never had to rely so heavily for glass and scientific instruments on a foreign power. The first action to rectify the glass shortage was taken by the Institute of Chemistry which considered the needs of the country with respect to chemicals, dyestuffs, glass and porcelain vessels. Though the institute's original concern was the production of laboratory glassware, it soon extended its production to other types of glass. Various departments at the NPL were engaged in work to alleviate the shortage. The Chemical Division began to investigate problems encountered in the commercial production of glass, while the Metallurgy Department carried out research on refractory material and the Optics Department undertook the testing of glass specimens with regard to refractive index and dispersion.

The Technical Optics Committee, appointed by the British Science Guild, was aware, nonetheless, that Britain would soon experience shortages of optical glass that would become so great that they would affect "almost all varieties of glass except for bottles and windows". Optical glass was needed most urgently for telescopes, binoculars, range-finders, prismatic compasses, gun-sights and periscopes.

By April 1915, Chance Brothers, still the only suppliers of optical glass in Britain, announced that it would in future supply material only to the manufacturers of optical instruments who could produce War Office or Admiralty certificates. Scientists writing to *Nature*, however, were concerned about this change as it meant that the whole of the optical industry in Britain would not be supplied with any glass whatsoever.

Early in 1915, Glazebrook wrote to four leading firms involved in the manufacture of optical and scientific instruments. He was then contacted by Walter Runciman, president of the Board of Trade, about the shortage of glass. Runciman supported Glazebrook's scheme for adequate funding of the manufacture of optical instruments, and the Treasury gave its approval for a grant for the work. Nevertheless, the funds which were made available were still largely inadequate to meet existing needs at the end of 1915.

The situation began to improve in the early part of 1916. One reason was that since the supply of optical instruments to the armed forces was of a cumulative nature, unlike other munitions, it was inevitable that the demand would diminish after two years. The efforts of Chance Brothers were also of great value – since the outbreak of the war, production had increased by four and a half times. The increase was accelerated and, by the end of the war, the supply of glass from Chance Brothers was more than thirty times the amount it had been in 1914. Though there had been much anxiety about relying on German imports, supplies of glass also came from the United States and Japan which eased the situation.

The work undertaken by the NPL had, in the end, a significant effect upon the production of optical glass and instruments. The Executive Committee of the NPL held the view that the shortage of optical glass need not have happened if funding had been available in 1900. It was also clear to the committee that future scientific research would demand a far greater financial commitment. Subsequently, it persuaded the Treasury that additional funding was needed, and this led to the formation of the DSIR in 1916.

CHAPTER 6

Financing War Work and Female Scientists at the NPL

During the First World War, it was the optical glass programme that involved the largest amount of original research at the NPL. Much of the rest of the work undertaken was of a routine nature and dealt with solutions to various problems on a daily basis. A month after the war began, and despite the amount of work that had to be done for the nation, 38 of the staff at the NPL were sent on active service. During their absence, the Executive Committee agreed to keep their posts open and to treat time spent with the colours as service at the Laboratory.

By October 1914, the Executive Committee of the NPL reported that it had an overdraft of £4,000. Its income had been mainly dependent on fees, but the war had modified this situation by the additional funding the NPL had received for military purposes. Though there were fewer salaries to pay since some staff had gone on service or had been transferred to government departments, the NPL was still having difficulties paying its employees. In a letter to the Treasury, Rayleigh expressed deep concern that unless assistance was obtained from government funds for the payment of salaries and the working of the Laboratory, the committee was faced with the probability of having to close the NPL down before the end of the 1914 financial year. Rayleigh pointed out that such a course of action would be disastrous to the future of the Laboratory. After 14 years in existence, the increasing worth of the work was becoming more and more apparent to the government: the necessity for the application of science to industry was daily becoming more obvious.

In the first two months of the war, the NPL assisted the War Office and Admiralty in researching, "several critical cases of grave importance".

This work included tests on gun-sights for ships and aeronautical work; the resources of the Froude Tank had also been called upon by both the Air Department of the Admiralty and the Construction Department. The Executive Committee of the NPL estimated it would need about £22,000 from October 1st 1914 to March 31st 1915. The situation eased somewhat when the Committee for Scientific and Industrial Research was created on June 21st 1915, which led to the creation of the DSIR one year later. Parliament then provided the NPL with £25,000 for the financial year 1915-16.

The NPL's independent efforts in undertaking war work began in 1915, when Sir Richard Paget of the Admiralty wrote to Glazebrook suggesting that the Laboratory should become involved with "experimenting in technical improvements of the services". The Ministry of Munitions, established in 1915, enjoyed a close relationship with the NPL. Some of the work the NPL undertook for the Ministry involved the accurate calibration of the gauges widely used in munitions manufacture to check the dimensional precision of components. This gauge-testing was an area of particular importance to the munitions industry, and certainly the NPL had sufficient expertise to relieve the overworked Inspection Department at Woolwich. The gauge-testing was carried out in the Metrology Department: during peacetime, the Laboratory had tested about 1,000 gauges per year, but in 1915 alone there were more than 50,000 gauges to test. The Ministry of Munitions decided to stop testing at Woolwich and to transfer all work to the Laboratory.

Women at the NPL

Near the end of 1915, the NPL's Executive Committee considered the idea of employing women for the first time, but some members of the Executive Committee thought this would lead to objections on the part of some of the gauge-makers and the scheme was dropped. However, in keeping with contemporary trends of women working throughout Britain, just a few months later, in response to increasing demands from the Munitions Department, women were enlisted. Through the insistence of the Executive Committee and Glazebrook, women were given equal pay to men from the outset. The NPL welcomed them heartily and hoped that their experience would be pleasant, although the men who were serving abroad initially had misgivings about such "revolutionary proceedings".

Once the women began working, the demands placed on the Metrology Department for gauge-testing were resolved, though it soon became clear that a new laboratory would have to be built to house the work undertaken for the Munitions Department. By June 1916, the Metrology Department had tested 132,000 gauges, and by the summer of 1917 it was testing as many as 9,000 to 10,000 gauges a week. By then, 99 out of the 420 staff were women, but when the war ended the majority of these women were replaced by men returning from the forces, as was

Mine testing during the First World War.

Gauge testing building.

the case throughout Britain. Nevertheless, the Laboratory never reverted to being the all-male establishment it had been before the war.

Eventually, virtually all of the departments at the NPL became occupied with war work. The Froude Tank was used for naval testing, the Heat Division carried out experiments on heat loss from surfaces, and the Electrotechnics Division became involved in test work and instrument design. Aeronautics research continued to enjoy its privileged position. In November 1915, the Treasury asked the NPL to double its Laboratory staff for aeronautical experiments. Although two new wind tunnels and several buildings had been erected by 1917, the newly-formed Air Ministry wanted the NPL to increase still further. By the end of the war, aeronautical research had grown so considerably that nearly all divisions of the NPL were involved with it to some extent.

Funding for the wide range of war work came from various sources. The Treasury continued its small annual grant-in-aid, and the Admiralty and the War Office gave additional funds for specific projects. The Ministry of Munitions was responsible for financing gauge-testing, and the Committee for Scientific and Industrial Research sponsored various programmes at the NPL.

Relations with the Committee for Scientific and Industrial Research were first established after Rayleigh and Glazebrook had contacted it regarding some of the NPL's research programmes. They pointed out that within the work of the Laboratory, there were several items which fell within the scope of the committee. It was hoped that the committee

Two views of clinical thermometer testing, 1914.

might make a grant towards one or more of these important investigations. Consequently, financial aid was allocated for work on light alloys, the heating of buried cables, hardness testing and heat flow between surfaces and optical glass.

The ease with which these funds were obtained aroused a discussion concerning the overall financial position of the NPL. Rayleigh then wrote to J J Thomson, the president of the Royal Society, that the NPL was continually in difficulties because the scale of pay to the staff was not high enough. Rayleigh was becoming convinced by the idea of the Royal Society becoming associated with the Privy Council Scheme. As one member of the NPL's General Board saw it, the NPL could become a government department with the Royal Society as its manager. The board approved of this structure and thought negotiations with the DSIR should be opened in the belief that such an association would "further the promotion of an organisation of scientific research throughout the kingdom".

CHAPTER 7

The Department of Scientific and Industrial Research

In the aftermath of the First World War, scientists regarded Britain's failure to match its chief commercial and military rivals to have been a result of the neglect of science by successive governments. The critics accused them of having failed to "make use of the best scientific advice available". Before the war, the most influential organisation engaged in promoting the claims of science had been the British Science Guild whose goal was to promote scientific research as having an essential role in industrial development.

There had been other organisations addressing these national concerns. When the Imperial College of Science and Technology was founded in 1907, it aimed to provide the "fullest equipment for the most advanced training and research in various branches of science, especially in its application to industry". Like the NPL, Imperial College was in large part a national effort. By this time, the mechanical science laboratory founded by Professor James Stuart at Cambridge in 1885 had grown into an important department of engineering, and similar departments had been established at universities across Britain. Moreover, numerous technical colleges had been set up, notably in Glasgow, Manchester and London.

The government's response to the pressure of scientific opinion was one of greater flexibility. There was a recognition that it would not be enough to simply develop more effective resources for research, but that it was of paramount importance to increase the manpower capable of undertaking the research. In May 1915, William McCormick, as chairman of the Advisory Council, formed a committee to investigate the matter. It was this committee that pointed out that the expansion of industrial research was primarily dependent on a continual supply

Staff of the Metrology Division during First World War.

of scientific manpower. At the same time, the presidents of the Boards of Trade and of Education received a deputation from the Royal Society and other learned societies urging government assistance for scientific research for industrial purposes, and the establishment of closer relations between the manufacturers and scientific workers.

In June 1915, the Liberal government made way for the creation of the coalition ministry, and in July the new president of the Board of Education, Mr Henderson, issued a white paper outlining the government's scheme to establish a permanent organisation for the promotion, organisation and development of industrial and scientific research. Such a body was to operate nationally and devise the most effective means to undertake the necessary research. While the necessity for central control of the machinery of war had been obvious for centuries, the need for uniting military and industrial effort in Britain had not been generally understood until the First World War revealed the consequences of this lack of unity.

When McCormick was writing his report in August 1916, he expressed the view that the experience in Britain at that time led people to think that the small scale of British industrial firms was one of the main impediments in the organisation of research. McCormick also thought it was essential for British firms to take a more direct interest in foreign competition: it would be impossible for the state to support them if they failed to take such an interest. He also urged that universities must be the

Physics and Aeronautics staff 1917.

main source of research in pure sciences, as discoveries made in such institutions often had wider practical and technical applications.

Although the Royal Society administered an annual grant of £4,000 from the Exchequer in aid of particular researches at the NPL, and the Treasury gave £7,000 towards its upkeep, the Advisory Council of the Royal Society recommended a further grant for equipment and other research at Teddington. The NPL had by then been drawing part of its funds from the Treasury for its original work in physics, engineering, metallurgy, research into ships, aerodynamics, electricity and metrology.

The first task facing the Advisory Council was to assess the nature and magnitude of the problems involved in encouraging the development of industrial research. Enquiries were made into the number and distribution of staff and postgraduate students in institutions of higher education, whose ranks had been severely diminished by the war as the majority had either entered the armed services or had been recruited by the Ministry of Munitions, the Admiralty or the War Office.

By August 1915, the Advisory Council was promoting 20 projects including: research into optical glass; refractory materials; the properties and composition of alloys; the corrosion of non-ferrous metals such as tin and tungsten; and the setting and disintegration of salts and crystalline substances. A number of professional institutions carried out the research in various laboratories such as the NPL, in private laboratories and in academic institutions (including Imperial College,

Manchester and Sheffield Universities).

A number of the largest steel manufacturers, threatened in the early months of the war with the exhaustion of supplies of chemical glassware, made contributions for research on a co-operative basis at the NPL. The Institute of Chemistry had by then set up a Glass Research Committee under Professor Raphael Meldola of University College London. Following the DSIR's Advisory Committee's encouragement, Professor Herbert Jackson discovered a process for manufacturing a number of types of glass necessary for testing material and products.

On the assumption that it would have been impossible to improvise an effective system at the moment when hostilities ceased, careful consideration was given to the problem of ensuring the persistence and growth of industrial support for applied research after the war. A comprehensive scheme was needed for securing the more general acceptance of the co-operative principle in "the difficult period of reconstruction which followed the war".

From September to December 1916, plans for providing assistance for industrial research were worked out in greater detail. It became increasingly apparent that the implementation would not only require the provision of financial support on a greatly increased and expanded scale, but also that the administration would involve a complex system of central co-ordinating machinery.

The pressure for movement in these directions culminated in the statement by Lord Crewe to a deputation from the Board of Scientific Societies on December 1st 1916. Sir J J Thomson introduced the deputation and stressed, "the necessity for further grants in aid of research both in pure science and in its application to industry". In reply, the Lord President Haldane of the council announced the government's intention of forming the Department of Scientific and Industrial Research (DSIR). After the DSIR had replaced the Committee for Scientific and Industrial Research, the Royal Society appointed a small committee consisting of Glazebrook, Rayleigh and Sir Alfred Kempe "to consider the best mode of carrying into effect the suggested association of the NPL with the DSIR's Advisory Committee of the Privy Council". Both Glazebrook and Rayleigh favoured a far higher degree of commitment by the state to the cause of science. Glazebrook, in fact, expressed the view that the NPL should be financed entirely by the government since the laboratory's work was of a national character.

The Advisory Council remained under the Executive Committee of the NPL, but as the nucleus of a new agency, it was to be able to develop its interests more fully. Subsequently, the Advisory Council planned to advise on a "proposal for establishing or developing special institutions or departments for the scientific study of problems affecting particular industries or trades". Two of these "special institutions" involved the National Physical Laboratory and the Chemical Research Laboratory. From 1916 to 1918, the Advisory Council of the DSIR had to deal with many requests for scientific advice in the solution of war-

Visit of King George V, 1917.
top *talking to Walter Rosenhain.*
bottom *with Sir Richard Glazebrook.*

related problems, and the NPL was frequently called upon for various solutions.

The DSIR takeover of the NPL

When preliminary discussions between the government and the Royal Society began in 1917 regarding the future of the NPL, the Royal Society proposed that the DSIR should undertake responsibility for the finances of the laboratory and that the NPL staff should become government employees. Control of the Laboratory research programme was, however, to remain in the hands of the Executive Committee.

The NPL staff thought that every indication suggested that the government would continue to make excessive demands that stretched the resources of the Laboratory – not just for research needed by the fighting services, but also for research on problems arising in the civilian industries which desperately needed an injection of modern science. There were differences of opinion about how extensively the government would require the assistance of the NPL. One factor influencing the timing of the DSIR takeover of the NPL was Glazebrook's impending retirement in 1919. The DSIR clearly wanted to make use of his 20 years of experience when it came to negotiating the conditions under which the NPL staff would be directed scientifically. However, serious disagreement between the NPL and the DSIR arose on matters of scientific control.

CHAPTER 8

Conflict and Control

The sources of the NPL's war work emphasised to the government the importance of fostering scientific research. With the creation of the Department of Science and Industrial Research (DSIR), it appeared that the government had accepted the burden of such responsibilities. Disagreement, however, eventually arose between the Royal Society and the DSIR: the Royal Society wished to retain its role in naming future directors of the NPL while the DSIR believed that its financial control must necessarily govern the scientific management of the laboratory. The DSIR could not, however, make any claims for its competence in the area of scientific research as at this time no members of its headquarters' staff were research scientists. Moreover, the part-time scientists on the DSIR's Advisory Council did not have the time to become involved with the administrative matters of the NPL.

Serious disagreement over the basic principle of who should control the research policies of the NPL led to inevitable conflict over policy, finance and responsibility. As Eric Hutchinson has observed, in spite of the NPL's role as a national metrology laboratory, the Laboratory under Glazebrook and the Executive Committee had taken on a distinctly academic atmosphere, much like that of a large, modern university physics department.[9] The cultivation of a scholarly atmosphere was a deliberate policy of the Executive Committee, which expected the NPL staff to move to and from universities. Glazebrook emphasised this view in a letter he wrote in 1916 to Frank Heath (secretary to the DSIR from 1915-1927) stating that the NPL staff who were of "the higher grades correspond to lecturers and junior professors in the universities, while the superintendents ranked with the professors who were heads of departments in universities". This academic feature was also evident in the pension schemes for the staff, which were invested in the Federated

Superannuation Scheme for Universities. So, though the staff were to become government employees, they were not to be regarded as civil servants.

Glazebrook and Heath were the two main antagonists in this debate about control over the NPL. Glazebrook wished the president and council of the Royal Society to have scientific control of the NPL, while Heath favoured the transfer of the institution to the government. The council of the Royal Society regretted that these changes, proposed by Heath, were not compatible with what they had understood – namely, that the society should retain all aspects of scientific control.

The Executive Committee proposed grading and salary schemes for employees of the NPL, ensuring that women received the same salaries as men, as Glazebrook had insisted when women were first employed at the NPL. The DSIR eventually and reluctantly accepted these proposals, but refused in later years to extend them to other laboratories such as the Chemical Research Laboratory. The salaries were by no means extravagant. At the top end of the scale were superintendents who received £800-£1,000 per annum, and at the bottom of the scale were junior assistants who were paid £175-£235 per annum and were expected to hold university degrees in science. By contrast, the starting salary of a junior administrator civil servant with a BA degree was more than £500, while a first-class clerk without a university degree earned £250.

The leadership of the NPL began to realise that when the war ended its finances would inevitably return to their previous critical situation, primarily as a result of salary problems. This brought home the immediate advantage of absorption by the DSIR. With a fundamental agreement reached between the Royal Society and the DSIR, the department then approached the Treasury. When the Treasury replied ten weeks later, it had overlooked the fact that its grant-in-aid had always been made to the Royal Society and not directly to the NPL.

Glazebrook continued to express his disquiet over the form the new administration would take. Before the war, financial constraints meant that the Executive Committee was unable to offer salaries commensurate with the value of the work undertaken as gauged by salary scales elsewhere. As industry slowly began to realise the advantages of pursuing its own scientific research, it was becoming increasingly common for workers on the staff at the NPL to leave for greater financial reward. As the trend continued during the war, Glazebrook remarked that the salary which industry could offer the NPL was "at least double those which the Executive Committee is able to give".

The NPL had encouraged a flow between the Laboratory and industry. The Executive Committee considered not only that NPL staff should go out into industry, but also that scientists working in industry should be attracted to working in the NPL. However, the salaries which the NPL could offer were no longer sufficient to either retain the most capable staff or to attract men from industry. Such was the magnitude of the problem that by 1916 resignations among senior members were becoming embarrassingly frequent. It was now very clear that the thorny question of salaries required urgent attention.

A protracted and bitter correspondence occurred between Glazebrook and Heath on this issue. Glazebrook asked repeatedly for some definite action to take place regarding salaries and the numbers of established posts before the takeover. Heath stonewalled repeatedly, requesting detailed information on the minutiae of overtime pay from Glazebrook. Ostensibly, the DSIR was planning to approach the Treasury for temporary salaries. Heath had proposed overtime payments based on pre-1914 salaries. In turn, Glazebrook dismissed Heath's suggestion by pointing out that the staff were being paid in 1918 and not in 1914. In any event, it seemed to Glazebrook that Heath's "elementary algebra was mathematically faulty". The morale of the NPL staff was in serious decline owing to a number of unintelligible delays in funding.

Apparently, the Advisory Council of the DSIR was in complete agreement with the aims of the Executive Committee. The council considered it to be of the highest importance that the financial position of the laboratory staff should be improved and that scientific works should be well remunerated. Meanwhile, the Chancellor of the Exchequer, Winston Churchill, had already given his approval for the transfer of NPL property and income to the government as suggested by the DSIR. The Treasury then gave its consent to the department proposal and the transfer was to date officially from April 1st 1918. But the proposal (which was not subject to negotiation) was presented to the Executive Committee after the takeover date and without adequate explanation. Heath then approached Lord Southborough (who had been elected to the Executive Committee in 1916) in an attempt to calm the angry reaction that Southborough had provoked. Southborough replied that, "the pundits were beginning to think that the Royal Society should get out and leave the laboratory to become a government department."

Nevertheless, there was a delay in implementing the new salary scales. Despite the Advisory Council's promise to recommend salaries for the scientific staff which would not be less advantageous than those proposed by the Executive Committee, the NPL thought that negotiations were prolonged over an unacceptably long period. The DSIR then claimed that Glazebrook had not disclosed sufficient information about the salaries currently paid. Subsequently, the DSIR informed the Treasury that the department was no longer in a position to make any proposals for temporary provision of salaries. When the official date of transfer passed, no announcement was made concerning future salaries. It was thus no surprise that the newly formed National Union of Scientific Workers became strongly represented at the NPL.

By early July, the forbearance of the Executive Committee was exhausted. By then, the NPL staff had been employed by the government for two months, but still had no reliable information about the salaries they were supposed to receive. Glazebrook began to put increasing pressure on Heath. Being very much aware that the work of the gauges and aeronautics staff was widely recognised as being of first-rate importance, he highlighted the danger of losing members of the two teams through delay in implementing the new salary scale. He wrote to Heath: "the urgent work we are called upon to do cannot be done because the staff cannot get the salaries for which provision has been made." Glazebrook then added that General Bingham, the controller of Munitions Design, had told him that the NPL's work had saved the war situation as far as the supply of gauges was concerned.

Glazebrook warned Heath of the Executive Committee's unrest. Moreover, he said, the NPL staff needed to be reassured that they would be no worse off than was indicated in the original scheme. Finally, Heath began to understand how deeply he had offended the Executive Committee. He realised that unless two points in Glazebrook's letter were satisfied, then certain members of the committee were likely to make a public announcement of their resignation. Confronted with the probability of public disclosure of the scandalous delays, the secretary of the DSIR, Frank Heath, and McCormick met with Sir Thomas Little Heath of the Treasury and acquiesced that the Executive Committee scheme be accepted.

Although the dispute over salaries had finally been settled, relations between the Royal Society and the DSIR, especially with respect to the matter of control, were strained. It was generally accepted by the Royal Society representatives that the Executive Committee should retain full power of control to secure the efficient working of the laboratory. The issue of scientific freedom in the management of the NPL was crucial. Eventually, members of the DSIR were outclassed and outmanoeuvred by the scientific competence of Southborough, who had become the spokesman for the Royal Society. As a former government finance officer, Southborough was able to counter the claim that the Treasury would automatically refuse to put funds at the disposal of the Executive Committee. The DSIR then accepted that the concession proposed by Lord Curzon would have automatically terminated at the end of the war. Curzon then suggested that the financial administration of the Laboratory should be reviewed after the war. At that time, the Royal Society and the Executive Committee of the NPL were to be consulted to determine any future polices. Though this procedure saved face for the DSIR, the freedom of the Executive Committee was, in fact, never challenged until the Ministry of Technology directly absorbed the NPL in 1964.

CHAPTER 9

Industry and Physics

The cessation of hostilities in November 1918 had naturally caused a large reduction in the amount of work done by the Laboratory for the War Department, especially gauge work undertaken for the Ministry of Munitions. The NPL had, in fact, been supporting a substantial number of testing research programmes for which there was now no further need. Some projects associated with military requirements continued as before, particularly those included in the aeronautics research programme such as the light-alloy research. In addition, there were investigations in the Froude Tank Laboratory into mines, torpedo firing and submarine defence. Also, the aftermath of the war meant that whole branches of science had to be added to the Laboratory's programme including X-rays, radioactivity and wireless telegraphy. New advances in illumination and electricity as well as acoustics and noise were all integrated into various departments at the NPL.

One of the great developments brought about by the war was a more systematic standardisation and testing of manufactured products in the interests of the export trade as well as of the home consumer. New ideas, developed for service requirements during the war, were also leading to the establishment of new industries which necessitated, in turn, the establishment of new areas of research at the Laboratory.

During the inter-war period, British industry became more responsive to scientific expertise. Various factors affecting the rate and direction of the development of science during this time included: the uncertain economic climate during the 1920s and 1930s; the growing concern among scientists with the organisation and application of their work; and the change in status of the scientist. Inter-war Britain was characterised by the decline of the older, established heavy industries such

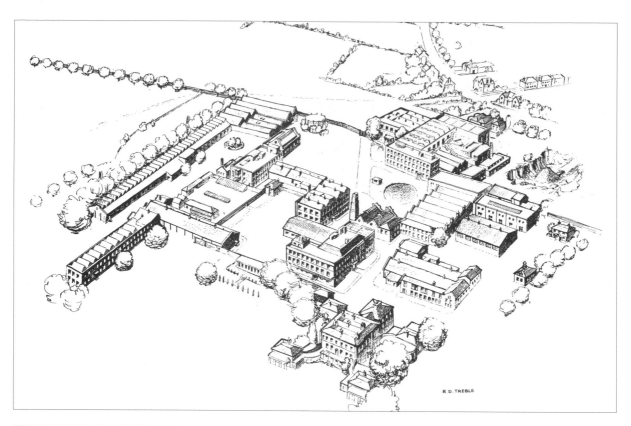

R.D. TREBLE

Carbon ring furnace 1919, an early high temperature resistance furnace.

as heavy engineering and shipbuilding, and the growth of new science-based activities. New industries emerged such as: radio, electrical power generation and transmission, non-ferrous metallurgy, aeronautics, motor engineering, motion pictures and the manufacture of synthetic polymers such as rayon. Two other new industries which emerged during the inter-war years were electricity supply and transmission, and light alloys (for aeronautics and new metallurgy).

During much of 1918 and 1919, Glazebrook was involved with placing the Laboratory on a secure peacetime footing. Before his retirement in September 1919, he wished to see a resumption of basic research and the extension of the NPL's activities. One of the ways he sought to achieve this was in the establishment of local laboratories throughout the country in an attempt to relieve the NPL of the burden of much of its routine testing. Glazebrook favoured a Birmingham branch of the NPL for gauge-testing, along with other provincial stations for chemical glassware testing and certain types of electrical work. It was hoped that this scheme would enable the Laboratory to concentrate on more interesting industrial research.

Glazebrook had also wanted to extend the Laboratory activities by further testing and standardisation of electrical equipment. In the spring of 1918, a committee appointed by the Institution of Electrical Engineers put forward a scheme for a British electrical proving house. The committee consisted of members from the DSIR, the Board of Trade

Two aerial views of NPL.
top *1920.* **bottom** *1919.*

77

*Thermometer testing, early
1920s.*

and the Office of Works. The purpose of the proving house was "to examine and test within ordinary commercial limits all classes of electrical appliances to approved specification". If Glazebrook's second plan had succeeded, it would have provided the NPL with a large amount of basic research work in electrical matters. Unfortunately, Glazebrook did not receive unanimous support for the proposed project, at least not in its original form.

Frank Heath not only disapproved of the NPL's proposed involvement with the scheme for industrial work, but also of Glazebrook's plans for local testing centres. Heath objected that these new developments were intended to deal with commercial products which he felt the NPL should not be involved with. Glazebrook pointed out that the NPL had always undertaken commercial work. The DSIR, however, felt that sufficient commercial testing bodies already existed, for example the Manchester Chamber of Commerce Testing House for the cotton industry.

In early 1919, a ministerial decision was made on the matter of commercial testing. In line with the DSIR's recommendation, it ruled against associating the NPL with either of Glazebrook's proposed schemes or with any similar organisation in future. Instead, this should be the responsibility of the Board of Trade. Although it had been agreed in principle that the scientific control of the NPL should remain with the Royal Society (as opposed to the Executive Committee), the DSIR's veto over the proposal of the Executive Committee showed that in practice the DSIR had the power to decide what work the NPL would undertake. A certain amount of routine commercial testing, nevertheless, continued to be done at the NPL.

Glazebrook's retirement

On September 18th 1919, Glazebrook retired as the first director of the National Physical Laboratory, bringing to a close 20 years of intense personal involvement with the development of Britain's first national laboratory. On his retirement, he returned to live for a time at Cambridge but later returned to London to Notting Hill Gate, and in 1924 he built himself a house at Limpsfield Common, Surrey. He continued to serve on various committees at the NPL till 1932. Glazebrook, probably more than anyone else, was concerned by the possible dangers that could arise if the NPL's work was directed by the DSIR. He had wanted to preserve the autonomy of the NPL's Executive Committee, which had been managed by the Royal Society. Such autonomy was, however, elusive and would have been difficult to sustain owing to his own retirement as well as Rayleigh's departure from the chairmanship of the Executive Committee. Moreover, the unsatisfactory economic climate of the 1920s, which deeply affected the work the NPL undertook, only served to underscore the loss of control by the Royal Society.

By the end of the war, the DSIR had been managing the NPL for seven months. Despite the protracted arguments with the Executive Committee, in the hands of the DSIR the work undertaken by the NPL was becoming more germane to the general public. Moreover, after the war Whitehall had realised just how significant the contribution of science had been to the war, and this led directly to the government initiative of providing a fund of £1,000,000 for various research departments of the DSIR. When the engineer and physicist Sir Joseph Petavel was appointed director in 1919, the work of the Laboratory extended into a number of new fields to meet the needs of industrial applications that depended on the rapid progress of physical science.

Taxi-meter testing, 1920s.

Before Petavel took up this post, he had worked at the Davy-Faraday Laboratory at the Royal Institution, where he established the primary standard of light, and designed an indicator for measuring pressures set up in exploding gaseous mixtures which later became known as the Petavel Gauge. With his background in engineering, Petavel leaned towards the pursuit of short-term work for industrial utility as opposed to longer-term speculative research, to which the DSIR responded very favourably. Under Petavel's direction, the Laboratory also became involved in practical projects that affected the daily lives of the British public. Petavel is also remembered for the beautifying of Bushy House and its grounds in which he planted many bulbs.

Illumination and lighting

When the DSIR had set up its sub-committee of the Physics Investigation Board in 1920, problems of illumination and lighting were pursued in a number of directions. (By then, the principal subjects in the Department of Physics included matter, heat, light and sound.) A joint committee was appointed to look into the lighting of public buildings. In 1921, a large number of measurements of existing illumination conditions were made in textile mills in Lancashire and Yorkshire. The committee also dealt with the lighting of rooms for massed clerical staff. It had

Lamp testing.

been decided that, from the point of view of economy, comfort and ease of maintenance (for both fittings and decoration), semi-indirect lighting was the most satisfactory solution. One of the clerical rooms for which it provided the lighting was in the Pensions Ministry Building at Acton, west London.

Other experiments on the daylight and artificial illumination of buildings included determining the most suitable illumination for picture galleries and museums (including the Science Museum and the British Museum). Investigations were also made to determine the most suitable coloured glasses for signal lights for ships, railway and aircraft. Illumination problems were regarded as being of great national importance, as they affected the health and safety of the public in their homes,

*Portable apparatus for the
measurement of signal strength,
1925.*

public buildings, vehicles, streets and open spaces. In 1924, the Laboratory
was called upon by the DSIR to undertake illumination research for
the entire nation.

Acoustics and sound

Before the war very little attention had been given to research into
sound, either at the universities or elsewhere. Owing to pressure of
other matters, the NPL's work on sound had been limited to a few tests
of tuning forks and the Galton whistle (a high-pitched whistle devised
by Sir Francis Galton, cousin of Douglas Galton, which only dogs could
hear). During and following the war, the subject had grown in national
and industrial importance. Acoustical methods were used for various
reasons by the fighting services during the war, and this knowledge
was subsequently adapted for other uses, such as surveying and signalling
at sea. A Sound Division had been added in 1922 and by 1927 the NPL
realised that more work needed to be done in connection with the
acoustics of buildings. Another application came with the availability and use of the telephone, gramophone and broadcasting, which
gave the study of sound transmission problems worldwide importance.
Occasionally, the Sound Division worked with the Buildings Research
Board. An important programme of work for the board included investigation into the wind forces on roofs and structures, the vibrations of
buildings, the expansion of concrete and the acoustical problems of
the Royal Albert Hall.

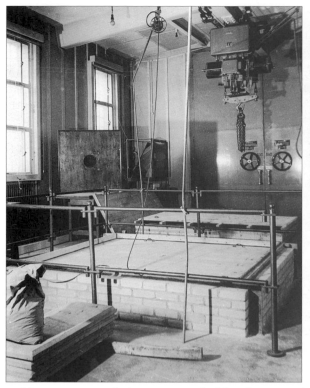

New accommodation was needed for the acoustics division in the Physics Department due to various electrical and mechanical interferences from passing trains. The acoustical work was partly housed at the top of Victoria House but this was becoming an increasingly unsatisfactory situation. In Victoria House the conditions were such that vibrations produced by the passage of heavy vehicles in the adjacent road, or even by people walking in the building, affected amplifiers and galvanometers so seriously as to render it doubtful how far their experiments with precision acoustic measurement could be pursued. Moreover, the proximity of Elm Lodge, with its high-frequency electrical furnace, X-ray discharges and spark gaps, resulted in the reception of electrical disturbances so powerful as to swamp completely the effects in which the staff were interested when using electrical methods of measurement for acoustical work. There was clearly a need for more suitable and adequate accommodation of sound research on a different site with better isolation.

left *Upper transmission room in the Acoustics Laboratory.*
right *Million volts sparks in air produced at the rate of 100 per second by the high voltage power frequency generator.*

Food Investigation Board

The work for the Engineering Committee of the Food Investigation Board dealt with the pressing importance of the problems of cold storage, with a view to the preservation of the thousands of tons of food which were annually lost through decay before they could be marketed. One of the first projects involved work on the insulation of refrigerated structures. Following this came the investigation of air

83

High voltage equipment.

circulation among stacked boxes in cooled enclosures. In 1921, the
NPL had established a working relationship with the University of
Cambridge and was able to proceed with the erection of a low-temper-
ature research station on a site provided by the university.

By 1929, the work of the Food Investigation Board involved the
following activities: refrigeration systems; heat insulation materials;
and instruments and methods of measurement for use in connection
with food preservation. Its investigations led to results of considerable
interest and importance, and helped materially in the intricate problems
connected with the transport of food, in particular of meat, fish and
fruits.

Reduction in funding

The expanding amount of targeted research resulted in the stretched
resources of the NPL being deployed away from more general research.
If finances could have accommodated these demands, then all aspects

*Section of the 3.2 kV transformer
showing the driving shaft
operating interstage sphere gaps.*

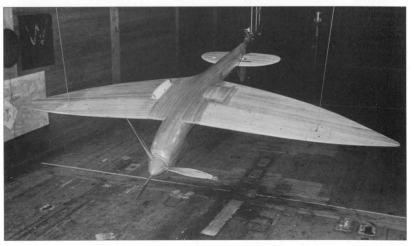

of the work at the NPL would have received the attention each warranted. However, the pressure exerted by the Treasury on the DSIR ensured that any monetary increase was highly unlikely during the First World War. When the short-lived post-war economic boom came to a halt in the early part of 1921, demands were made for economies and deflation. The government appointed the Geddes Committee in 1921 to make recommendations for further reduction in funding. The committee proposed drastic cuts of £75 million in the overall budget for government expenditure affecting all areas of national life. Nevertheless, military aircraft continued to receive high priority in funding. The government eventually decided upon a cut of £64 million.

In this financial climate, the Treasury adopted an even more critical view of the DSIR's expenditures. The Executive Committee had requested £245,574 for the financial year 1921-22 – much to the chagrin of the Treasury which thought that such a request was, "worse than in the days of Sir Richard Glazebrook to whom all last year's failings were

above *Models of the Gloster VI plane (suspended and inverted for wind-tunnel testing) , 1929. It was designed to compete in the Schneider Trophy contest.*

top *Seaplane Supermarine Napier, 1926.* **bottom** *Model of a seaplane, 1930.*

ascribed." Under the pressure of the Treasury, the DSIR's Advisory Council suggested a reduction in the overall estimate for 1921-22 of some £20,000. Any such reduction that the DSIR could make naturally pleased the officials of the Treasury. The withdrawal of £20,000 from the NPL was achieved by cutting back the general research and standards programmes, since a commitment to work for government departments had already been made. As far as the Treasury was concerned, the NPL ought to have been capable of obtaining sufficient money from routine work to assist it in pursuing various research programmes (i.e. self-financing research).

In the worsening economic climate of the early 1920s, the Treasury continued to make further reductions across various government departments. From 1921 to 1924, the government's cuts meant that the NPL's estimates of expenditure had been reduced by over £70,000. As the Treasury's retrenchment began to take effect, the Royal Society set up a research committee for the Laboratory in 1922. The three most prominent members of the committee were Ernest Rutherford, J J Thomson and William Lawrence Bragg, whose mission was to lobby the cause of basic research, but the committee experienced only a limited degree of success in its campaign.

The Treasury continued to shape the policies of the DSIR by limiting the budget. In 1926, the Treasury's financial secretary, R MacNeil, wrote to Winston Churchill, Chancellor of the Exchequer, saying that if he had his way with the NPL, he would "wipe it out as a separate department with its £300,000 of salaries, its £20,000 of travelling and its £1,700 of telegrams and telephones", though MacNeil offered no alternative scheme nor replacement for the NPL. Fortunately for the NPL, Churchill was not entirely sympathetic to MacNeil's ideas. While Churchill agreed with some of his views, he pointed out that the Prime Minster, Stanley

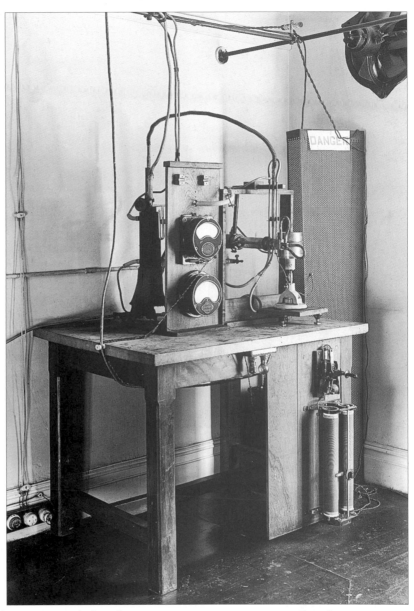

Apparatus used in the application of X-ray methods to industrial problems.

High voltage laboratory.

Director's office in 1932.

Baldwin, supported the new policy of the NPL and thus: "The idea of spending money boldly on research is one for which many arguments can be adduced." The Treasury, and MacNeil in particular, only grew more hostile towards the NPL during this time.

Despite the many new advances in physics and the new knowledge it provided in X-rays, radiation and wireless telegraphy which, in turn, produced new industries, the Treasury was reluctant to invest any more money. Nevertheless, in June 1928, the NPL submitted a scheme to the DSIR for the provision of new buildings. In addition to the High Tension Electrical Research Building and the Physics Building, the scheme proposed a photometry building and a building for acoustics as well as accommodation for standards work. Relations between the NPL and the DSIR in the late 1920s were at a particularly low ebb. Things were to become worse before they improved, as Britain entered another cycle of economic depression from 1930-1935. The Treasury subsequently further reduced expenditure in all government departments. During the depression, basic innovative research received little attention from the government, and even later, when trade began to pick up and industry became more active, it was the DSIR's Research Board and Committee which received priority over the NPL's Executive Committee and its suggestions. Moreover, the effect of the severe trade depression

Absolute voltmeter, 1951.

had been felt in all branches of industry.

The rapid change of directors at the NPL during the 1930s did not help its position. In 1932, when Glazebrook was 76 years old, he retired from the chairmanship of the Executive Committee; he died three years later. One year later, Sir Joseph Petavel, who had been the director since 1919, also died. Sir Frank Edward Smith, who had been employed at the NPL since 1900, became its acting director following Petavel's death. In 1937 Smith was replaced by Sir William Lawrence Bragg who left after only ten months at the NPL to take up the chair of experimental physics at the Cavendish Laboratory in Cambridge. In 1938, Bragg was succeeded by Sir Charles Darwin, grandson of the famous evolutionary theorist, who remained director until 1949. Darwin's administrative talents were demonstrated by his reorganisation of the Laboratory before and after the Second World War. His main contribution to science was his theoretical research in optics and particularly in X-ray diffractions, atomic structures and statistical mechanics. These rapid changes not only broke the links with the early years of the NPL, but also prevented the implementation of any long-term coherent plans for future developments. By the late 1930s, the financial situation at the NPL was very similar to what it had been just before the First World War.

top left *Sir Frank Smith.*
top right *Dr (later Sir) William Lawrence Bragg.*
above *Sir Charles Darwin.*

CHAPTER 10

Military and Industrial Research

Despite the generally unfavourable climate in the 1930s, British industry did become more scientific in its outlook and began adopting scientific methods and skills. Thus, new buildings were constructed at the NPL. The Physics Building was completed during the early part of 1931 and was shortly afterwards occupied by the section of the department formerly working in Bushy House. The rooms vacated in Bushy House were fitted up as a conference room with an adjoining committee room. The Acoustics Building had finally been approved and construction began in 1932. Proposals were submitted for a new Photometry Building and for further facilities for the Froude Tank research.

Radiology

Work in the Radiology Division, a section of the Physics Department, had been growing and continued with a view to establish the Röntgen – the international unit of X-radiation adopted at the Stockholm Congress in 1928 – as the working unit for intensity measurements in industry in the UK and around the world. Interesting results had been obtained in the application of X-rays to various industrial problems. Improvements in technique had been developed which had dealt with the examination of micro-structures of tungsten steels for magnets and transformer cores, and the relation of grain size to hardness in steels.

The application of X-rays for medical therapy and diagnosis had greatly increased by 1930. In 1934, the Medical Research Council requested the assistance of the Radiology Division for further X-ray studies of the structure of tooth enamel. The X-ray work suggested a classification by various types of selective crystal orientation which

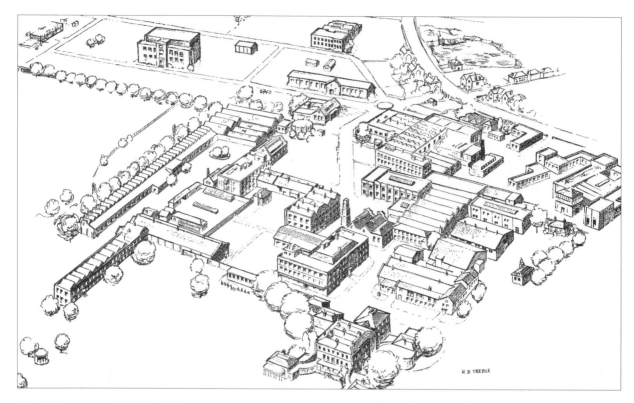

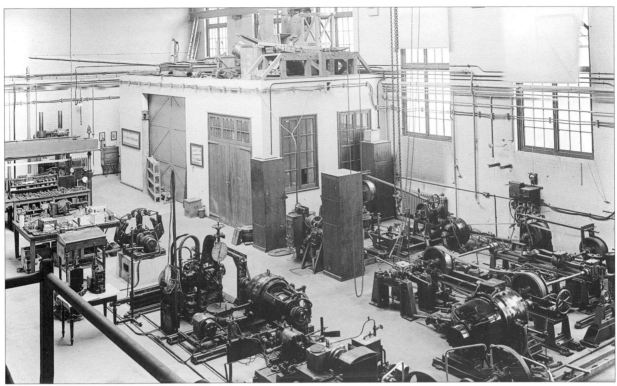

characterised the enamel and distinguished it crystallographically from the underlying dentine.

Main Bay Engineering Building, 1932, showing fatigue and other testing machines.

Radio research, acoustics and metrology

Immediately before the Second World War, a scheme was prepared and approved for the formation of a wireless department at the Laboratory. In the early 1930s, a Radio Research Station was established by the DSIR and a Wireless Division was constructed at the NPL to co-operate in this work. By 1933, radio direction finding on short waves had been pursued and the experimental conditions had been ascertained for the reduction of errors in the observed bearings. Considerable attention had also been given to the production and propagation of ultra-short waves. In the following year, the Executive Committee was invited to include the Radio Research Station at Slough within the organisation of the Laboratory.

It was agreed that this could be best accomplished by the formation of a separate department, under a supervisor, to deal with all the wireless experimental work carried out both at the Laboratory and at Slough. The Radio Department was subsequently created and Mr R A Watson-Watt, formerly in charge of the Radio Research Station, was appointed as superintendent of the department. The station at Slough was situated, by permission of the Admiralty, in the grounds of the Admiralty Compass Observatory at Ditton Park. A sub-station was also located at Leuchars, Scotland, used principally in the inves-

Aerial views of NPL.
top *1930.* **bottom** *1932.*

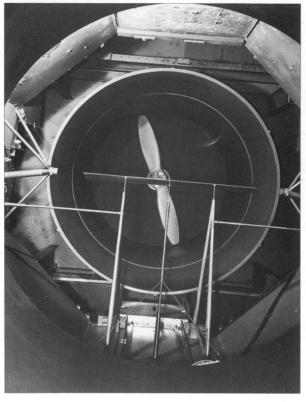

tigation of atmospheric interference.

By 1934, there were six million radio licence holders in Britain who spent £3 million annually on licence fees and approximately £40 million annually on sets and accessories. The income of the BBC comprised £1,300,000 in net licence income (with an additional £300,000 from publications). The Post Office earned £300,000 per annum for its collecting, controlling and engineering services in regard to the radio licence, though, ironically, none of this money went to the NPL. Throughout the 1930s, the programme of research in the Radio Department was mainly concerned with the propagation of radio waves and its relationship to practical problems of communication and direction-finding. The more important aspects of the research dealt with the design and calibration of the Adcock system of direction-finders and the design of a short-wave visual direction-finder employing a cathode-ray tube.

Eventually, the increasing complexity of industry's demands on the services of the Laboratory called for the provision of additional equipment installation, requiring further floor area – although it was not thought to be necessary to increase staff in the same proportion. While it had not been possible to expand the facilities at the Laboratory during 1933, due to the depression, effort had been made to press forward with the Executive Committee's research programme. The erection of the first part of the Acoustics Building was completed in 1933. The Laboratory was now divided into seven departments: Physics (including heat, optics, acoustics and molecular physics), Electricity, Metrology (measurement of length, area, volume, mass and time), Engineering, the Froude Tank Laboratory, Aerodynamics and Radio.

For some years, the Metrology Department had been making preparations for the determination of the yard and the metre in terms of the wavelength of light. Preliminary results were announced in 1932 when the length of the material standards defining the yard and the metre had both been determined in terms of the red wavelength radiation of a cadmium spectral lamp.

Science and industry

One of the areas in which the NPL continued to work in close alliance with industry during the depression was through its investigations into sound and acoustics.

Physics Building, 1931.

During the 1920s and 1930s, the general public had become increasingly noise-conscious. Many factors had contributed to this, including the introduction of broadcasting, the mechanisation of the workplace and the intensification of road traffic.

Alongside these developments, building methods had changed as the solid brick-built residence housing a single family and affording fairly complete isolation had given place to large blocks of buildings of light construction. Noise was readily transmitted in these blocks from one residential unit to another unless adequate precautions were taken. Similar changes in industrial buildings had taken place increasing the general noise level. By 1938, modern electrical devices such as the microphone, valve amplifier and oscillograph had replaced the orthodox equipment of the pre-war acoustical laboratory. Moreover, precise definition and measurement of sound and of acoustical properties of material had become possible.

By 1937, the Executive Committee regarded it as a matter of primary concern that the facilities available at the NPL should be devoted to giving industry the scientific assistance necessary for its advancement. The committee also stressed that the programmes of research, investigated under the supervision of the committee, would be reviewed periodically to ensure that, in the widest sense, the work was of benefit to the country. An important aspect of the work undertaken at the Laboratory was the investigation of problems put forward by industrial firms and by representative bodies such as the Research Association.

top *A view inside the compressed air tunnel.* **bottom** *Wind testing tower with a model of SS Mauritania on top.*

High Voltage Building, 1928.

top *Testing of motor horns.*
bottom *Measurement of noise, 1932.*

Firms which experienced difficulties of a technical nature were invited to communicate with the director of the Laboratory, who could let them know if the NPL was in a position to offer any assistance. Some of the specialised areas included: precision measurements, fracture in metal, refrigeration, lubrication, colorimetry, fluid flow, acoustics of public buildings and the application of X-rays to industrial problems.

The routine testing of instruments formed an important link between the Laboratory and industry. In addition to the assurance given by a Laboratory certificate or report that an instrument met the standard of calibration required, the Laboratory was often able to help the manufacturer with suggestions for improvements in accuracy or reliability. The methods of mass production used in the 1930s depended for their success on the accurate mass manufacture of individual parts. To secure consistent results, components had to be made to specified dimensions within certain defined controlling limits of accuracy: this was achieved by the use of appropriate gauges at various stages of manufacture. This need first arose on a large scale during the First World War when methods were evolved at the Laboratory for the testing, and in some cases the production, of gauges required for munitions purposes.

The role of the NPL during the wars

Since the First World War, industry had made increasing use of the facilities provided by the NPL. The demands for accuracy had become more exacting, to such an extent that the Laboratory was increasingly asked to carry out tests with a degree of accuracy that would never

have been contemplated in previous decades. The rapid advances in the use of very high frequencies in radio work, particularly in connection with television, necessitated the determination of the properties of electrical insulating materials at these frequencies. It was the NPL that found that many materials exhibited properties at high frequencies which were markedly different from those found at lower frequencies.

There were a number of ways in which the Laboratory assisted industry during peacetime. In 1936, the NPL determined the thermal properties of refrigeration materials at temperatures below -40° F, the heat loss from a hot-water cylinder and the ventilation of an operating theatre. It also measured noise, assessed the wind pressure on chimneys and roofs, and measured the viscosity of cream. A number of questions in connection with acoustical insulation in buildings and the suppression of vibration were also dealt with.

By 1939, it had become clear to one observer that the potential of the NPL in the inter-war years had not been fulfiled and that its contribution to the welfare of industry had been limited. Writing in 1939, the physicist John Bernal remarked that routine work, though important, occupied too much of the NPL's

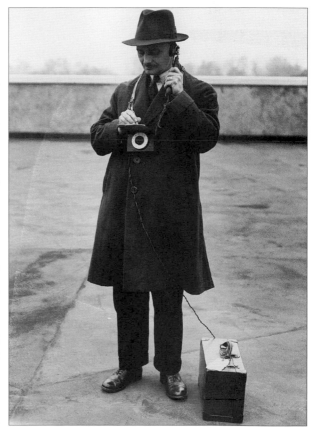

Testing lubrication oils in the Lanchester worm gear machine, 1920.

time. He thought the NPL should be concerned as much with the discovery of new possibilities as with the remedying of old defects. Bernal pointed toward the aerodynamics and wireless sections, where new processes and positive developments were directing the considerations.

In the first half of 1939, the NPL followed its normal course of work, directed towards its four main functions: the assistance of industry in its immediate problems by advice and experiment; the research of a

Experiment showing the airflow over a ship's superstructure using a plume of smoke, 1956.

longer-range programme, which aimed to open up new technical possibilities to industry; the testing of instruments; and the maintenance of standards on which all physical measurement depended. With the outbreak of the Second World War, an entirely new state of affairs arose. Circumstances had changed significantly since 1914 when the Laboratory was far smaller. It held a unique scientific position as a national organisation which placed innovative research, rather than technical developments, in the forefront of activities.

As the First World War had progressed, the NPL had begun to deal with problems connected with aeroplanes and submarines as well as with the gauges used in the manufacture of munitions. During the intervening 25 years, the Laboratory had expanded to four times its original size to meet the demands of an industrial system which had itself established research laboratories on a very large scale. Moreover, each of the three services (armed, fighting and military, as they were then known) had also created a strong research department to deal with its own particular problems. The consequence of these changes meant that there were again problems arising out of war conditions.

Nevertheless, Britain was far better prepared for war in 1939 than it had been in 1914. There were no critical shortages of material that could be attributed to a lack of scientific research. Optical glass, despite a decline in the fortunes of the industry in the inter-war years, was available in adequate quantities – the lessons of the First World War had been well learned by the Optics Division. The only problem concerning optical glass supplies was that of variety: an adequate supply could only be obtained by concentrating attention on a small number of glass types which manufacturers had been urged to adopt as far as possible. However, the resources of the Laboratory were not

Vacuum spheres for use with hypersonic tunnel, late 1940s.

used at once, as several other institutions also existed. In particular, the research laboratories of all three branches of the services absorbed much work. At the start of the war, the NPL decided not to allow any dispersal of the scientific staff. Routine advice continued to be given, as did help to industry, while much of the work previously done for the services expanded considerably.

Until 1941, most sections in the NPL were able to continue much as they had before the war, and civil industrial research continued to receive attention. For example, routine measurements, both for the maintenance of Laboratory standards and for the testing of instruments and measuring appliances, formed the bulk of the work of the Metrology Department. The investigations carried out in the Radio Department, on behalf of the Radio Research Board, were directed to three main objectives: the study of the production and propagation of ultra-short waves; the development of the technique of direction-finding for waves of about two metres; and the study of the ionosphere and mode of propagation of radio waves.

Continued progress had been made in the Aerodynamics Department with the programme of research under the direction of the Aeronautical Research Committee, and work had also been carried out for the Air Ministry and the Admiralty. The incidence of work for the Services had, in fact, fallen unequally on the nine divisions of the Laboratory. The Metrology and the Radio Departments had absorbed the majority of staff transferral from other departments. However, the Engineering and, to a lesser extent, the Aerodynamics Departments had also shared in the redistribution. Staff now employed on work for the services had continued with the general research and maintenance programme of the Laboratory.

Digging air raid shelters in 1938. Trenches were dug at selected points round the NPL by staff and some buildings were sandbagged. The trenches were later replaced by reinforced concrete tunnels.

Air raids and bombs

When air raids by the German Luftwaffe started in the late summer of 1940, there was for a time considerable interference with the work of the Laboratory as staff were sent to shelter in the extensive trench system. On several occasions, bombs were dropped in the Laboratory grounds at night and generally fell in places where little damage resulted, but on the night of November 29th 1940, a more serious raid took place. Two medium-sized bombs fell in the main roadway causing much dislocation of services and considerable damage to windows. Another bomb damaged the largest of the new wind tunnels, and a large bomb which failed to explode fell close to the new tank and interfered seriously with work in this part of the Laboratory.

Damage as a result of a bomb on 29 November 1940.

The unexploded bomb that lodged under No 2 Ship Tank in 1940. Although photography of this sort of subject was forbidden during the war, photographs of damage at the NPL still turned up.

War work

During 1940 the number of departments increased, owing to the inclusion of the Department of Light. This comprised the former Optics Division of Physics and the Photometry Division of Electricity. The work of Optics consisted of the study of the design of optical instruments, glasses, polarisation and standards of colour measurement. It also undertook a large amount of test work on field glasses. The work of Photometry involved the study of light standards such as the exact value of the international unit of candle-power, qualities of electric and other lamps, illumination and problems of vision. It gave advice and conducted experiments on problems of lighting in factories, rooms and streets. The Optics Division continued to examine scientific instruments for the Admiralty. By 1941, a large number of special investigations had been undertaken for the services concerning the influence of veiling glare on the precision of range-finders; the effect of low-reflection lens coatings (blooming) on the performance of binoculars; and the influence of temperature on the optical properties of telescopes.

Routine thermometer tests showed an increase. The number of clinical thermometers tested during 1940 was 820,000 compared with 764,000 in 1939, while the number of precision thermometers tested rose from 10,300 to 12,600. The increase in numbers for the latter was mainly attributable to the large demands for thermometers for

meteorological work and for explosives manufacture. In the Electricity Department, work for the defence services included the production of devices for the detection of delayed action bombs.

As the demands of the services grew, the NPL's basic research along with industrial work of a non-military nature diminished. This was true even of metallurgy, one of the most dynamic areas of the NPL in the inter-war period. The one area which was able to maintain a significant commitment to basic research was aerodynamics. Advances made in fundamental aerofoil research led to a significant increase in aircraft performance. Aeronautical progress, as in the First World War, was rapid, and the existing research facilities at the Laboratory and elsewhere had been hard put to meet all demands.

By 1941, all departments of the Laboratory were working for the defence services. Moreover, in most departments the whole of the time of the staff was being devoted directly to the war effort. The NPL's director Charles Darwin was seconded to the position of director of the Central Scientific Office British Supply Council in Washington DC to improve Anglo-American scientific war co-operation. He stayed for six months. Edward Appleton, secretary of the DSIR from 1939-49, acted as director of the NPL during Darwin's absence. When Darwin returned to Britain, he was made scientific advisor to the Army Council in addition to continuing as director at the NPL. In 1943 he resumed his full-time duties at the Laboratory.

CHAPTER 11

Reorganising the NPL

During 1942, steady progress was made in all departments of the Laboratory for the war effort. The increased demands on the services of the Laboratory were once again met mainly by the recruitment of women. In addition to clerical duties, they took on work as laboratory assistants and laboratory mechanics. Much of the observing, calculating and testing work was undertaken by laboratory assistants. By 1943, there were 210 more women and 29 fewer men at the NPL than there had been in 1939. The majority of the newly recruited women (115) were laboratory assistants and most of these were in the Metrology Department. The total number of women employed at this time was 413. Many of these women stayed on after the war, some holding key positions right into the 1980s.

The gauges tested in the Metrology Department on behalf of the Directorate of Ammunition Production were stored at the Laboratory, and at various sub-stores around the country. For security reasons, a proportion of each type of gauge was stored at two of the sub-stores as well as at Teddington. The testing and re-testing of worn or damaged gauges was conducted on a 24-hour basis, so that firms involved in war work received replacements with the minimum possible delay.

Sound and Light Divisions

By 1942, the work of the Acoustics Division was almost exclusively devoted to investigations for the services. Some of the work undertaken included: underwater noise measurements; calibration of microphones and hydrophones; and the response characteristics of intercommunication telephone equipment for aircraft use. The silencing of aircraft engine test benches had also been investigated.

Polishing sections of metals for examination under a microscope, 1942.

The problems investigated by the Light Department in connection with the properties of the atmosphere included: the transmission of light in air at different levels; the extent to which aeroplanes scattered light; the amount of light reflected from clouds; and the conditions which affected the visibility of targets from the air. Methods of scanning the sky for the detection of hostile aircraft had also been addressed. The effect of the war had been to raise to high importance the understanding of human vision at low brightness levels. This had given rise to an entirely new kind of photometry. The first step had been made in the standardisation of scotopic vision to measure the response of the dark-adapted eye.

One major problem concerning vision related to the plastic screens of aeroplanes which scratched easily. In these circumstances, pilots were often unable to see clearly through their screens, particularly at night. Another interesting group of problems involved the rapidity of ocular reactions. It was, for instance, important to know at what time in the approach of an enemy aircraft a searchlight should be switched on to ensure that the plane would be seen practically immediately.

Radio-location and radar

From 1942 until the end of the war, the work of the Radio Department was directed wholly to service problems. Much of this work was classified as secret and details were not included in its annual reports and a further category of papers marked "secret" with a correspondingly restricted circulation was introduced. The Radio Department was closely associated with investigations into the propagation of very short waves through the atmosphere. The work on direction-finding problems had covered the whole range of wavelengths from 30,000 metres down to less than one metre. Members of the staff frequently visited service stations and establishments, giving advice and active assistance in the

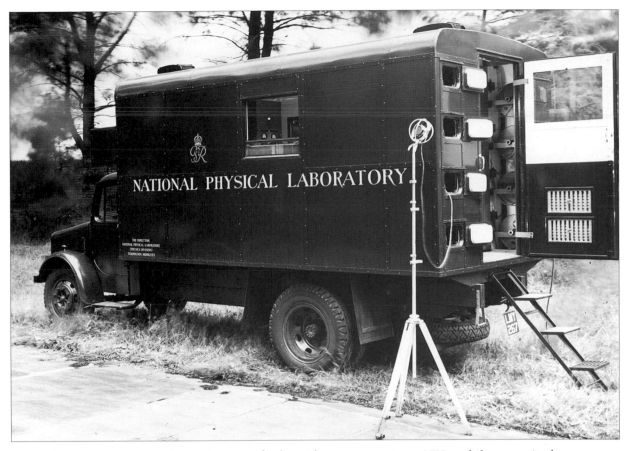

NPL mobile acoustical laboratory, late 1940s.

use and improvement of existing direction-finders. There were a very limited number of people in Britain with any specialised knowledge and experience in radio direction-finding, so it was necessary to place individual members of the Radio Department at the disposal of service establishments in a technical, consultative and experimental capacity.

The High Voltage Laboratory was mainly occupied with problems connected with radiolocation. High power modulators of the spark-gap type had been subjected to lifetime tests, principally to determine the most suitable material for the electrodes, and the effect on life of pulse length, pulse current and repetition frequency. Radar was one particular application of research carried out at the Laboratory which was to achieve universal fame. During the Second World War, it was claimed that radar, which offered a method of detecting the position of aircraft by bouncing radio waves off them, was the most important national asset to have emerged from the NPL.

By 1943, the demand for ionospheric information had increased. The prediction of the correct frequencies to use for various distances, at different times of the day and at various latitudes proceeded on a monthly basis for service use. Additionally, a continuous study was made of the propagation of radio waves through the ionosphere. In association with simultaneous direction-finding observations, methods

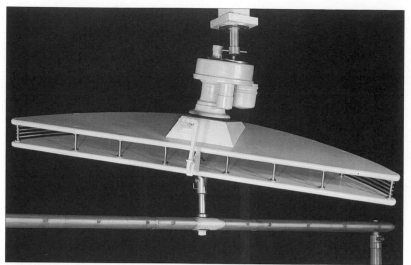

top *Admiralty radar reflector, 1956.* bottom *Radar scanner model in Duplex wind tunnel, 1957.*

were used to locate certain unknown transmitting stations from a single receiving station. Finally, work was done on the development of new directional finding equipment for use in ships on wavelengths or with aerial systems that had not hitherto been used.

Darwin's post-war plans

As early as 1943, the secretary of the DSIR wished to ascertain the views of the directors of the Research Stations associated with the department on its post-war policy. As director, Darwin was opposed to the creation of a ministry of science, since, "every single other department of state would consider itself compelled to be as unscientific as possible!" He remarked that while the DSIR covered the areas of inorganic science fairly well, there were undeniable gaps in the biological sciences. Though the Medical Research Council covered human biology and the Agricultural Research Council encompassed agricultural and veterinary science, Darwin wondered if the DSIR would consider the creation of a research station for biological work.

The maintenance of contact with industry was considered one of the most immediate problems for the directors of all the DSIR stations. Darwin thought that the difficulties faced in finding a suitable director of the NPL were threefold: first, he had to be a man of scientific foresight; second, he must be able to understand industry and convince industrialists of the value of the NPL; and third, he had to be very well organised. Darwin proposed that there should be more visits made by NPL scientists to industrial firms as well as to universities and overseas. He also wanted to see scientific attachés at the leading embassies in Washington DC, Paris and Moscow.

In assessing the future direction of the NPL in 1943, Darwin thought there should be about 1,000 employees of the Laboratory, with about 100 for each of the nine existing divisions. At the same time, discussions were also under way for the creation of a mathematics and statistics department (which later became the 10th division). Darwin thought it might be helpful to divide the departments into the following three classes: the standardising; those tied by geographical reasons; and those that happened to be in Teddington. Those departments in the first category consisted of Metrology, Electricity, Light and Physics. The tank at the William Froude Laboratory and Aerodynamics were part of the second category, while Engineering, Radio and Metallurgy fell into the third.

Darwin thought the NPL would benefit from using statistics and mathematics. With the growing awareness of statistical quality control of mass production, statistics was regarded as an area which "very definitely should concern the DSIR directly". It was expected that routine statistical methods would become well-established in industry (and indeed they have to the present day). The Executive Committee agreed that the subject of statistical research was particularly applicable to the Laboratory. Industry, during the war, had become "statistically-minded" *vis-à-vis* the subject of quality control.

During Darwin's secondment to the United States at the start of the war, he saw how statistical methods were used for quality control at the Bell Telephone Laboratory in Murray Hill, New Jersey. He wanted to put this to use at the NPL shortly after he returned. While the statistical methods used for industrial quality control had been devised by the English mathematician and statistician, Sir Ronald Fisher (in his agricultural work at Rothamsted Experimental Station in Harpenden), it was the American, Edward Demming, who implemented Fisher's methods for measuring and standardising quality control in industry.

There was also a strong case for the establishment of a mathematics station under the DSIR, capable of undertaking computational work, including both pen-and-pencil calculation and the kind done with arithmetical machines such as the differential analyser machine. This area was also intended to be capable of devising and making first models of new computing machines.

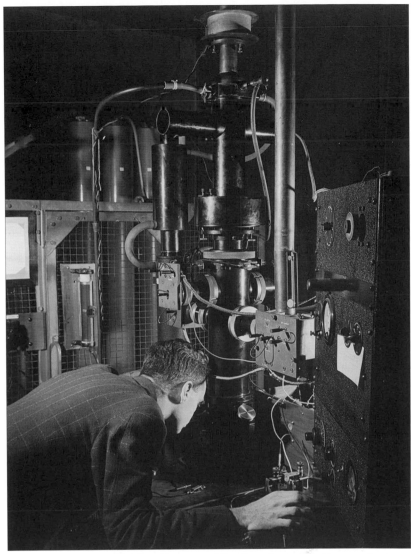

The first electron microscope to be installed in the Metallurgy Division, 1942.

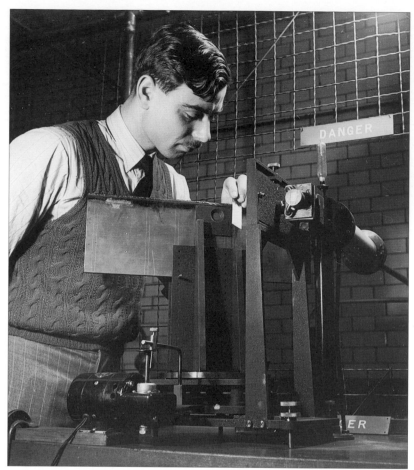

X-ray laboratory showing apparatus for measuring stresses in a weld in steel, 1942.

Demobilisation

The question of getting men serving in the armed forces back into civil employment was already under consideration in 1944, as the end of the war looked imminent. It was thought to be essential to give these men a period of retraining in the wider fields of science. Darwin considered the possibility of providing retraining by creating some ready-made employment at the NPL. The idea would be to take 30 to 50 men of the officer classes to work as assistants for a year or two. It was unclear how quickly requests for work from industry would return. In some of the NPL departments, there were large arrears of work to be caught up with, particularly in connection with the restoration and reverification of standards.

As to financing the scheme of retraining, it was recognised that the enormous payments for scientific work from the services would cease and that government departments, especially the DSIR, would have to carry the whole expense of the Laboratory, including salaries and an increased expenditure in connection with the restoration of equipment. Under these conditions, the payment of demobilised students was to be met from whatever provision was made for the general process of demobilisation. These men would not be taken on to the staff even in a temporary capacity, but would constitute a special category, which it was hoped would disappear entirely in the course of two years or so.

CHAPTER 12

The Advisory Council on Scientific Policy

Following the end of the Second World War, the services and supply ministries made fewer requests for assistance from the NPL. With the change to peacetime, the NPL was able to complete its existing investigations for the service departments. However, owing to wartime pressures and shortages of supply, there had been for several years little opportunity to maintain up-to-date equipment in the Laboratory. Consequently there was a pressing need for re-equipment in most divisions, and whenever feasible, the NPL made use of the government surplus stores.

Some of the most important war work the NPL had undertaken involved the organisation of the British effort in exploiting energy released in nuclear fission for the purpose of making an atomic bomb. In other directions, the DSIR carried out research into the construction and destruction of defence works and other structures, aircraft and ship design, radio propagation and other wartime devices. The DSIR thus referred to this as "the war of the physics of explosions". Another new wartime development at the NPL was research on "electronics", a term used to include investigations of the principles, design and development of electronic valve circuits and their very wide applications.

The experience of the DSIR before and especially during the war had shown the vast scope for the application of scientific methods to military problems. This had underscored the importance of the contribution that science could make to the solution of national problems. Scientists claimed that the war brought out the need to ensure the fullest and fastest application of available knowledge and new discoveries. For this purpose, a special Intelligence Division was added to the DSIR in 1945. Four years later, the Advisory Council for Scientific and Industrial

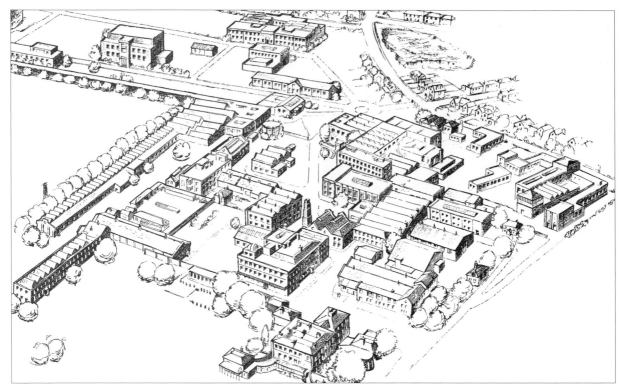

NPL site, 1940.

Research recommended that an intelligence section also be created at the NPL. It was to have the following aims: to make the work of the NPL better known to industry; to carry out surveys on scientific matters; to interpret to potential users the results of the Laboratory's work; and to establish contact between the Laboratory and scientific workers in universities, other research establishments and industry.

During the war, security requirements and pressure of work had caused individuals and small groups of staff to concentrate on their own particular jobs. Moreover, there had been very little interchange of knowledge of the various activities in the Laboratory between the staffs of the various divisions. As a result, the NPL experienced a serious loss of the power and effectiveness that had been previously derived from the breadth of its total fields of activity. By 1945, Sir Charles Darwin, still the director, decided that it was essential to reverse this tendency to isolation by scientists focussing on their own work.

Laboratory liaison committees

To establish a full interchange of information on the many phases of the Laboratory's work, Darwin set up the Laboratory Liaison Committee, which consisted of one representative from each division, appointed by Darwin. The general function of the committee was to plan and organise two different types of meetings. The first came to be known as "colloquia" and the second as information meetings. The colloquia were discussions on specific scientific subjects introduced by someone with specialised knowledge. The NPL organised 20 of these meetings from 1945 to 1949. The information meetings provided more general descriptions of the organisation and work of larger scientific units. Consequently, they were less technical and scientific and were aimed at all grades of staff. It was intended that all members of the staff could see how their divisions fitted into all the activities and laboratories at the NPL. Some of the meetings which had a general interest included, for example, industrial psychology. By 1949, the committee decided to establish the house journal, *NPL News*, as an auxiliary to its liaison activities. The first issue was printed on May 21st 1950.

During this resurgent period, Darwin also wanted to establish a line of communication between the NPL and other bodies. The Executive Committee thus, "unanimously agreed that contact with industry, government departments and the universities should be greatly encouraged in the post-war period." By then it had become evident to Darwin that there was a need to establish facilities for statistical research. Due to the increasing emphasis on industrial quality control produced largely by the demands of the war, industry was growing more receptive to the adoption of various statistical tools. The recent development in the direction of "automatic operations" coupled with Darwin's knowledge of various industries in the US which used statistical quality control methods, enabled him to see the wider applicability of industrial statistics at the NPL.

Automatic Computing Engine (ACE)

It was suggested that a centralisation of statistical work would increase the efficiency of computation and of accumulated experience, economise on machines and staff as well as encourage the development of new methods and machines. In 1945, the Mathematics Division was established at the NPL. A section was also created for the study of control mechanisms and John Womersley was appointed superintendent of the Mathematics Division. Shortly after being appointed, he followed Darwin's lead and made a visit to the United States to examine the various computers and calculating machines used at the Bell Telephone Laboratory, at Harvard University and at the University of Pennsylvania.

The seminal idea of automatic operation was present in the Hollerith punched card equipment, while the first machine capable of automatic operation was constructed by the International Business Machine Corporation (IBM) for Harvard University. It consisted of 72 adding machines, a mechanism for multiplication and division, three punched tape feeds carrying tables of mathematical functions, and a punched card for input and output. These various mechanisms were interconnected through what was virtually a small automatic telephone exchange: the instructions to the machines were coded in the form of perforation on a punched tape (also referred to as the "sequence control tape") which controlled the working of the machine. The Bell Telephone Laboratory had, since the end of the war, developed a series of machines

*ACE Pilot Model before
completion, 1950.*

known as relay computers with similar capabilities and of slightly higher
speed. They were constructed entirely of standard telephone relays,
the input and output of both numerical results and instruction being
on five-hole teletype tapes.

Womersley regarded it as self-evident that the replacement of telephone relays by radio valves would make transmission by higher speeds
possible. The Moore School of Electrical Engineering at the University
of Pennsylvania had already constructed a machine based on electronic counting for the Aberdeen Proving Ground. When these computing
machines were developed, plans were made for another machine, with
an even higher working speed, based on different principles, and
requiring less than one-tenth of the number of valves and other radio
components for the same performance as those used at the University
of Pennsylvania.

By 1946, Alan Turing had proposed to build the Pilot Automatic
Computing Engine (or Pilot ACE as it came to be known), which had
grown out of his work at Bletchley Park. It was intended that the
ACE machine would tackle whole problems instead of repeatedly using
human labour for taking material out of the machines and putting it
back at the appropriate moment. Turing estimated that it would cost
£13,000 to build. The Executive Committee reasoned that if such a

machine should exist in Britain "to keep up with world progress", then Teddington was its obvious home.

The Association of Scientific Workers

Darwin and the other directors of the DSIR research stations were not alone in formulating their views about the future of science and government relations in Britain. By the 1940s, it was recognised that the scientist was no longer a specialist in a narrow field who could remain aloof from the mainstream of administrative and executive matters. Though several programmes had been inaugurated during the war, including nuclear research, aeronautics and electronics, it was not until the end of the war that various attempts were made to formulate a policy for the future of science. In 1946, the Association of Scientific Workers (AScW) issued a report clearly bearing the stamp of Bernal. The report discussed the changes that should occur between science and government as part of the programme of general reconstruction.

The election of a Labour government in 1945 was seen by Bernal as a particularly favourable omen for the NPL. It was expected that the new administration would retain the co-ordination of resources established by the wartime coalition government and reject *laissez faire* as a national policy. The AScW's critique of science and government outlined three areas which emphasised the urgent need for a national science policy: the shortage of scientific manpower; the establishment of priorities in the allocation of finance and personnel; and the expansion of scientific work in previously neglected areas. The association had been critical of the government even before the war, as efforts tended to be directed toward remedying defects and failures rather than assisting in the positive development of science. Like Darwin, the AScW rejected the idea of a ministry of science and instead proposed a central scientific office, which would ensure that various sections of science could be spread throughout government. The aim of the central scientific office would be: to formulate policies; review work carried out by industry, government and universities; survey the output of scientific manpower; make financial forecasts; and safeguard scientists' rights of patent and publication.

An interim report for the Advisory Council on Scientific Policy suggested that "current fundamental research in the physical and biological sciences was unlikely to have any material short-term effect in increasing productivity". It was thought that the effective application of short-term results of scientific knowledge already available was likely to prove more fruitful. But the DSIR disagreed, since the effect of the war had been to divert effort from long-range fundamental research. It pointed out that during the war the government had relied on existing scientific knowledge and had done little to facilitate the development of new scientific ideas.

By 1945, an assessment of post-war needs by the DSIR indicated that there were several gaps in the national research structure which required filling. New research organisations were needed to provide a wider scientific basis for mechanical engineering development, which affected nearly all the national industries. The DSIR had decided to place the new Mechanical Engineering Research Organisation (later to become the National Engineering Laboratory) at East Kilbride, near Glasgow, and to set up branch laboratories of the Building, Fuel and Road Research Organisation nearby. Much of NPL's work on mechanical metrology and materials testing was transferred to Scotland to form the core of the new Laboratory's initial work programme. Additionally, there was a need to investigate civil engineering problems, in what was referred to as "loose boundary hydraulics", such as those associated with silting and scouring rivers and harbours, and coast protection. Problems of the attack of insect pests on stored food and other produce had brought about the creation in 1940 of a Pest Infestation Research Organisation. Negotiations with all departments concerned with radio communication led to a decision, at the end of the war, to establish a separate radio research organisation to absorb and develop the work of the Radio Division of the NPL.

Another development was in a transatlantic scientific liaison. Experience during the war of the value of the scientific mission in Washington DC, and the promotion of the exchanging of scientific information for the Ministry of Production, led to the organisation of the United Kingdom Scientific Mission, North American branch. There was also a unit of the British Commonwealth Scientific Office in Washington DC.

At the second meeting of the Joint Committee of the Advisory Council for Scientific and Industrial Research on January 11th 1949, Darwin remarked that any consideration of the future policy of the NPL must become largely a consideration of the relevant effort which the Laboratory must make regarding its three main types of work. These were: test work; special investigations for industry and for other government departments; and general research and maintenance of standards (i.e., research carried out at its own expense). The latter also involved the maintenance of the fundamental and derived standards and advisory work for industry and the government.

Nonetheless, British industry remained unwilling to undertake much-needed work, with the result that the only research carried out on a significant scale in certain areas was that undertaken in universities. The Advisory Council on Scientific Policy was aware that the country's economic difficulties were "largely due to 'technical backwardness' in large sections of British industry, and particularly their failure to exploit the results of scientific research".

CHAPTER 13

Applied Physics and Industry

By 1945, industrial productivity was being actively promoted throughout the country, and the Laboratory was considering the best way of giving the maximum immediate assistance in the solution of industrial problems. Since it was thought to be impossible with a limited staff to consider visiting even a representative selection of industrial firms, the NPL decided to send teams, each consisting of three or four scientific officers, to a number of research associations. These were set up by the DSIR to carry out applied research for specific industrial sectors and were part funded by subscription from their member companies. Each team was to spend about three days at a research association and then to report back to the Executive Committee. The plan was to engage some 14 or 15 officers full-time on the work for three months. By sending three teams away from the Laboratory simultaneously, it was hoped to complete a programme of visits to 20 or more research associations by the end of 1948.

Research associations visited by the NPL teams were involved with ceramics, cast iron, non-ferrous metals, paint and varnish, cotton, wool, leather, rubber, linen, iron and steel, food manufacturing and scientific instruments. Among the problems which were addressed during these visits were those concerned with the measurement and distribution of small particles, the measurement of temperature and viscosity (especially at high temperatures), the measurement and control of humidity and moisture content, and the estimation of cross-sectional areas, particularly in textile silvers.

Throughout 1948, every effort was made, in accordance with the directions from the Lord President of the Royal Society, Sir Robert Robinson, to improve liaison and contact with industry and to encourage

Testing the loudness and threshold of high frequency tones projected at observers in the form of plane progressive waves, 1954.

the effective utilisation of new scientific knowledge in the industrial field. In various other ways, attempts were made to secure more direct contact with industry. Hence an interdepartmental committee, known as the Panel on Automatic Control Techniques, was set up at the NPL to study the application of control methods, particularly those incorporating electronic devices. Discussions had also been held with various trade associations in an effort to broaden the field of calibration work which the Laboratory undertook on such articles as gauges and volumetric glassware. Manufacturers were encouraged to set up their own test sections under an arrangement whereby only occasional samples or control tests were necessary by the Laboratory. Attention had also been given to industrial problems associated with the Electricity, Light and Metrology Divisions. The international agreement to change over the electric unit from the old international to the new absolute values was implemented on January 1st 1949. The new photometric units were also introduced at the same time, and the change necessitated recalibration of a large number of Laboratory standards in terms of the "new candle", renamed the candela.

Darwin retired in 1949, and spent the last 15 years of his life devoted to problems of science and society. He became interested in the soci-

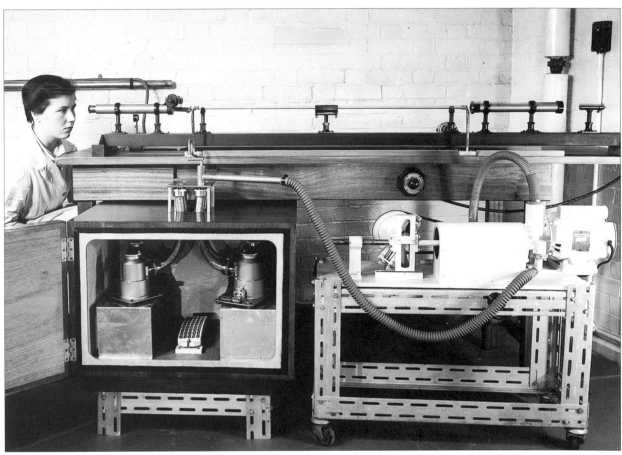

Testing of trichloroethylene inhalers used by mid-wives to administer trichloroethylene B.P. as an analgesic.

ological implications of the population explosion and became a neo-Malthusian. In 1952, he published *The Next Million Years* in which he considered the longer-term future of mankind. Darwin's successor, Edward Bullard, was a geophysicist whose scientific work was innovative. He was widely regarded as an inspiring supervisor and director.

The reorganisation of the NPL

The following three years saw the NPL undergo major reorientation and reorganisation in a number of divisions. In 1954, the DSIR visited the Laboratory, and shortly after this inspection, it received Treasury approval for a small expansion. Plans for the period 1954-9 were accepted, as was an annual staff increase. While any expansion by the DSIR was particularly welcomed by the NPL, *Nature* regretted that a major problem of the Laboratory was how to achieve maximum progress with an "inadequate staff" – inadequate, that is, in numerical terms.

By 1950, the volume of routine test work undertaken by the Laboratory had shown an appreciable increase. Considerable assistance had been given to scientists, technologists and industrialists in connection with a wide variety of problems. The advisory services of the divisions had always been an important part of the NPL, and there had been a

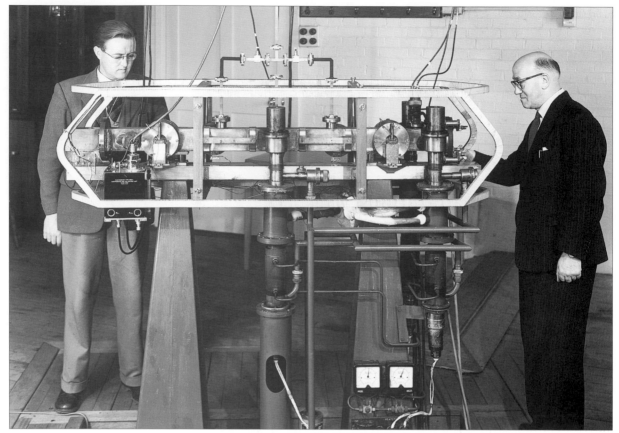

The original caesium resonator which led to the development of the atomic standard of time, with J V L Parry (on left) and L Essen, 1956.

steady increase in these services throughout the year. Advice had been sought for: the acoustics of a public address system in St. Paul's Cathedral; the acoustics of Winchester Cathedral; the evaporation of trilene in a device suggested for analgesia in childbirth; the temperature distribution within milk bottles during sterilisation; finding a possible method for locating leaks in buried water-pipes; the thermal and humidity problems involved in the subterranean growing of mushrooms; and the precautions to be taken when a radium needle burst open during sterilisation at a hospital.

Louis Essen and the caesium atomic clock

The NPL tests on timepieces were radically revised to meet the requirement established in 1950. A new test, known as the "craftsmanship" test, was formally introduced in March 1951 and replaced the "Kew Class A" test developed in 1884. The new test was designed to encourage the re-establishment of watch craftsmanship in Britain. Staff at the NPL also devised a new "sporting" test and revised the "stopwatch" test. Some four years later, in 1955, work on the atomic-beam standard frequency and time interval had reached the stage at which the first experimental model was in operation and was giving results of a precision never previously attained.

In 1950, Louis Essen, who joined the Electricity Division in 1933 to work with DW Dye, went to the National Bureau of Standards and the Massachusetts Institute of Technology to see the work being done on caesium atomic beams. Shortly after returning to Teddington, Essen proposed that an atomic standard should be adopted for frequency, thereby replacing the astronomical second with atomic time. Essen's caesium atomic-beam tube was the first apparatus to be used reliably as a clock providing time on a long-term basis. The indications were, however, that quartz clocks would remain the most convenient working standard and that it was worthwhile pursuing further investigations.

The ACE and DEUCE machines

The continued success of the pilot ACE model had a major influence on the Mathematical Division. The bulk of the work had been undertaken for the Ministry of Supply, and a number of aircraft firms had requested the use of the ACE machine. Typical jobs for the aircraft industry included: spar stress analysis; aeroelastic problems; analysis of the test-flight films; potential in unsteady flow; aircraft stability; fuselage cut-outs; pressure distribution on wings; analysis of kine-theodolite data; and many flutter calculations. Work for the Ministry of Supply on the reduction of noise from aircraft and from the aero-engine test house had also been continued.

In 1955, the Digital Electronic Universal Computing Engine (DEUCE) was installed. A start had also been made on the construction of the final Automatic Computing Engine (ACE). The possibility of applying computer techniques to clerical work was being considered in conjunction with the Ministry of Pensions and National Insurance. The Desk-machine Section continued to compute mathematical tables both for the Royal Society Mathematical Tables Committee and for internal use.

Changes at the DSIR

When the DSIR decided to expand the staff at the NPL, there was a feeling that some divisions had stronger claims to an increase in staff than others. With the introduction of 150 new posts initiated in 1953, the positions were divided between the Mechanical Engineering Laboratory, the Road Research Laboratory, the Water Pollution Research Laboratory, the Hydraulics Research Laboratory and the Fuel Research Station: all were considered for various reasons "most urgently in need of increased resources". In the following year, there was an increase in staff in other divisions which benefited the Aerodynamics, Ship Control Mechanisms and the Electronics Divisions. However, other sections of the Laboratory, which traditionally dealt with industrially oriented work, continued to suffer from a lack of personnel for some time. It had been possible to find a few posts to expand the Control Mechanism and Electronic Divisions, where support was readily given to the development of the full-scale ACE

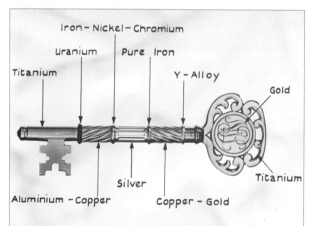

Iron – Nickel – Chromium

Uranium   Pure Iron

Titanium   Y – Alloy

Gold

Titanium

Silver

Aluminium – Copper   Copper – Gold

top *View of the creep laboratory in the Engineering Building, 1953.* bottom *Key used at the opening of the Metallurgy Building, 1954.*

and the application of electronic techniques to clerical work.

By the early 1950s, various divisions began to expand or renovate laboratories. Buildings were under construction for the Aerodynamics Division to house compressors and new wind tunnels for research into problems of high subsonic and supersonic flow, such as the determination of the characteristics of aerofoils with and without controls for high-speed aircraft. (The old wind tunnel building had been converted into a temporary lecture hall, and was used for information and scientific meetings plus a series of international symposia.) By 1953, the extension of the Metallurgy buildings had been completed and was occupied in early 1954. The new buildings provided improved facilities for work on ceramics, X-ray crystallography and the application of radioactive tracers to metallurgical research. Under the five-year plan for the expansion of the DSIR, the Laboratory had been allocated an increase of 70 non-industrial posts of which 20 were allocated during 1955, bringing the non-industrial complement to 790. Five industrial posts were also allocated (for a total complement of 276), and it was expected that a further 115 posts would be allocated in the following three years.

During this time, the relationship between government research stations and industry had become strained and caused much concern to both the NPL and the DSIR. (In addition to the NPL, other government research stations included the Forest Products Research Laboratory, Water Pollution Research Laboratory, Building Research Station, National Engineering Laboratory and the Laboratory of the Government Chemist.) The observed lack of government involvement was attributed to the Conservative administration's hostile attitude towards state aid for private industry. Such an attitude was consistent with the Conservative political philosophy of reliance upon private enterprise. The results of this policy soon became evident, as large sections of British industry remained unwilling to undertake essential work. The consequence was that the only significant research was undertaken in the universities, much as had been the situation at the end of the Second World War.

In 1955, the pharmaceutical chemist and industrialist, Sir Henry Jephcott set up a committee to review the organisation and functioning of the DSIR. The committee found that the direction of scientific effort was "inevitably inadequate to secure the most effective use of resources in the national interest". To give greater coherence to the policies of the DSIR, the committee recommended the abolition of the DSIR's Advisory Council and its replacement by an executive council for scientific and industrial research along the lines of the Medical and Agricultural Research Council.

In the following year, the recommendations made by Jephcott's committee were incorporated into the 1956 Department of Scientific and Industrial Research Act. The DSIR claimed that, with its reorganisation in 1956, "the experiment in organisation of government-sponsored scientific research that had begun 41 years earlier was completed." On the question of industrial research, the Executive Council admitted it was, "not yet ready to provide a precise answer". The council had also decided that the research stations, "should carry out pure research either to support their own work or to supplement the work of universities whenever that seems to be necessary or desirable."

Model of the Band I Section on the BBC television transmitting tower at Crystal Palace. The model was used in an investigation to determine the oscillating effects of wind on the tower, 1955.

Military research

As the Cold War developed, military research began increasingly to account for a significant amount of the nation's research and development funding, such that by the mid-1950s, 60 per cent of the total £300 million allocated annually was being used for military purposes;

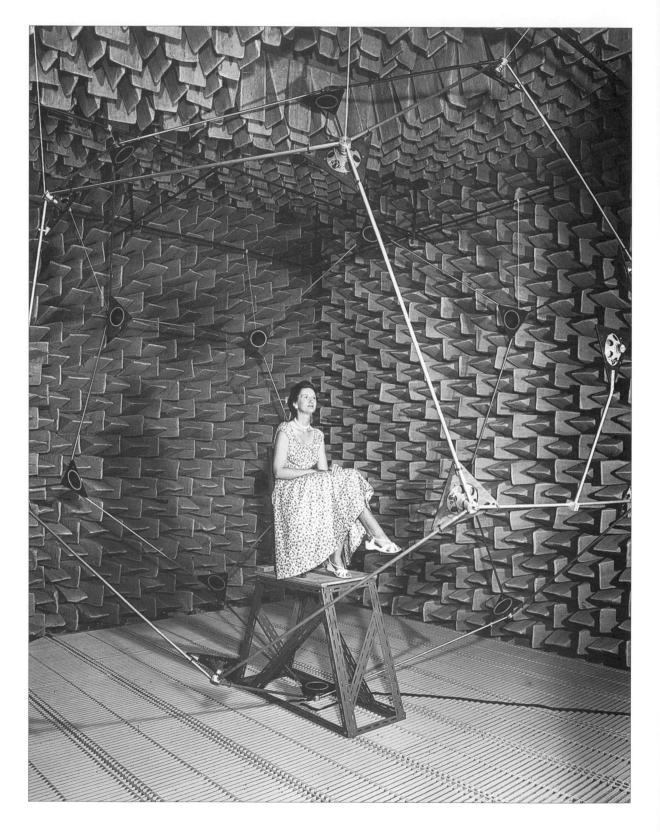

Darwin Building, 1955.

moreover, half of the scientists in Britain were engaged in this work, which had repercussions in the civil sector where resources were at a minimum. By the spring of 1955, Whitehall announced plans for future defence policies which entailed the reorientation of resources toward civil industry in an attempt to promote economic growth. A review committee was set up by the DSIR later that year to consider the organisation and research programme of the Laboratory; consequently, the NPL found its old structure modified. Two new sub-divisions were created for Physics, which consisted of Basic and Applied Physics. It was thought that industry would benefit from the work undertaken in applied physics.

The committee also considered and approved a proposal for the formation of a new research division at the Laboratory which combined the Electronics Division with the Control Mechanism Section of the Metrology Division. The fields covered by this new division were to be the automatic control of experimental, industrial and administrative operations as well as the development of techniques and equipment for data processing and computation. Much of the work was electronic in the sense that vacuum tubes were used, but the Metrology Division also included other devices such as relays, typewriters and teletype equipment. In fact, it included most light electromechanical devices, except for "electronics", in its radio and acoustical manifestations.

Subjective comparison of loudness of diffuse and progressive sound fields in an anechoic chamber, 1959.

The Laboratory was thus reorganised into nine scientific divisions: Aerodynamics, Control Mechanisms and Electronics, Electricity, Light, Mathematics, Metallurgy, Metrology, Physics (Applied and Basic) and a Test House. Through its sections which dealt with acoustics, radiology, testing heat and thermometry, high voltage and electrotechnics, the Applied Physics Division proved to be the principal source of aid for industry. It was given the "particular charge of giving assistance to industry and of bringing into practical use the precision in fundamental standard and the advances in basic ideas."

Nevertheless, the precise position of the Laboratory regarding its relationship to industry was still not clearly defined. With the removal of much military work, some progress had been made for civil industrial research. Certainly, the creation of the new Basic and Applied Physics Division was welcomed at the NPL. The difficulty experienced by the Laboratory's attempts to identify a well-defined role was exacerbated by the rapid emergence of new types of scientific work which led to new divisions being created. By 1952, the Executive Committee decided to relocate work on radar and radio research to the Radio Research Organisation and some of the engineering was transferred to East Kilbride.

CHAPTER 14

From Military to Civil Industry

The decision made by the Conservative administration in 1951 to undertake a comprehensive programme of rearmament had a far-reaching effect on the development of government-supported research institutions. With the onset of the Cold War, military research and development had remained at a high level, and defence spending had increased towards the end of Labour's term in office. As the profitability of British industry declined in the 1950s and the country fell into economic stagnation, it became clear that the government's rearmament programme could not be continued at its existing level. Equally, the reins of free enterprise constituted an unsatisfactory mechanism for sustaining economic growth. The overall results were a redirection away from military resources and towards civil industrial ends. These external influences greatly affected the post-war fortunes of the NPL. New types of work emerged while other traditional areas of research were lost.

By the end of the 1950s, the NPL began to turn its attention to civil industry. By then, the NPL realised that industry and science-based technologies were becoming ever more complex, and this led to a subsequent reorganisation and expansion of nearly all divisions at the NPL. While the role of civil industry continued to be of importance, military considerations still received high priority. The impact of this decision meant that, by the late 1950s, the NPL's industrial work was relying on

The Royal Commission on the Civil Service visits the NPL, 1954.

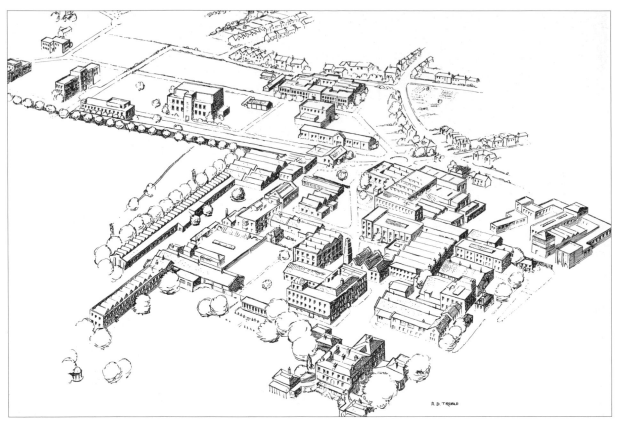

NPL site, 1950.

techniques of liaison and information that were hardly different from those used 20 years earlier. In 1939, there were 167 scientific officers and, by 1950, this had decreased to 165 – the scientific personnel strength at the NPL had barely changed since the beginning of the war.

Following the end of the Second World War, the superintendents of all divisions had interpreted somewhat rigidly the instructions to concentrate on items which were likely to be of immediate benefit to industrial productivity, and their original research work had suffered. The result of this policy was that there was not so much work of first-class scientific interest as there had been during the Second World War.

Basic research for industry was pursued in several divisions, notably those of Engineering, Light, Metallurgy, Metrology and Electronics and it seemed that the financial constraints imposed on the NPL during the inter-war years were to be lifted. Yet the Executive Committee still felt in 1951 that the increasing importance of the country's defence programme necessitated a review of the NPL's work. This would give the maximum assistance to departments working on problems that the Laboratory was best equipped to deal with. The emphasis on military work led to a noticeable change in the structure of the NPL during the early 1950s, a change accentuated by the transfer out of the Laboratory of two of its principal areas of research, engineering and radio, as more space was needed.

By 1956, most of the work of the Aerodynamics Division consisted

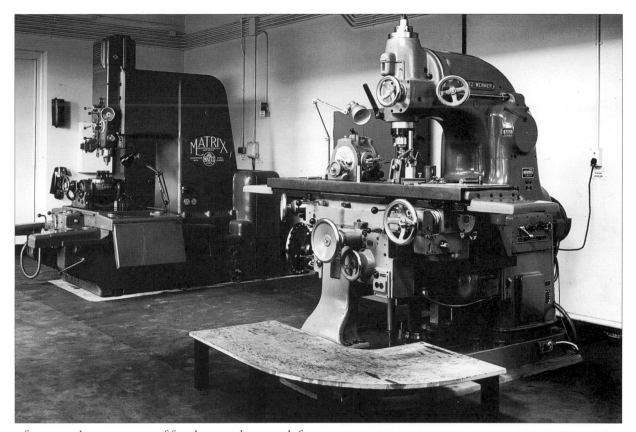

of a general programme of fundamental research for the Air Ministry. Close liaison was also maintained with the Royal Aircraft Establishment and the Ministry of Supply (which was the major procurement and R&D organisation for the forces), and consultation with aircraft firms took place frequently. Close contact had also been maintained with the Aeronautical Research Council and the Royal Aeronautical Society in addition to the Advisory Group for Aeronautical Research and Development of the North Atlantic Treaty Organization (NATO). Special attention was paid to problems of "mixed" flows at high subsonic, transonic and supersonic speed, and to schemes that would enable aircraft to take off and land vertically. The term

"mixed flow" was used to signify that flow was not always of the same type; thus, for instance, local regions of subsonic and supersonic flow could exist side by side.

Sir Edward Bullard resigned as director in 1957 and Dr Gordon Sutherland, who was named as the new director from September 14th, began to prepare a five-year plan for the overall development of the NPL. When Sutherland (who was at that time vice-president of the

top *Aerofoil workshop especially equipped for the manufacture of model aerofoils and wings, 1955.* **bottom** *Helicopter model in wind tunnel, 1957.*

left *Sir Edward Bullard.*
right *Dr Gordon Sutherland.*

Royal Society) became director, he brought an academic air to the NPL, emphasising basic research over less routine work. He believed the function of the NPL was to establish, maintain and improve standards of physical measurement, and to encourage, assist and where necessary to pioneer the application of physics in industry.

The total staff requirements necessitated an increase from 647 to 859 in the number of non-industrial posts. This led to some discussions with Sir William Lawrence Bragg and Sir Charles Darwin over what size the staff of the NPL should become. Bragg pointed out that the number of good scientists available was unlimited. Darwin did not think it was possible to determine the right size of the NPL and asked whether there was any branch of science at the NPL which could be "hived off". He thought it impractical to consider "hiving off" the Ship and Aerodynamics Divisions or to move the Metallurgy Division. Professor Whitehead, a member of the Executive Committee, remarked that expansion of the NPL was not unreasonable in the general climate of expansion of scientific work. Professor Wright Baker considered that an overall expansion of one third in the size of the NPL was about right. Sutherland commented that the Laboratory was concerned with the application of physics to civilian requirements. If military scientific work was to be reduced, as seemed likely, scientific and other staff should be available to provide for a limited expansion of the NPL. New staff were recommended for the Aerodynamics, Ship and Control Mechanism, and Electronics Divisions.

During this time discussions were held about the participation by the DSIR in the great expansion of radiological work which was taking place at Harwell in conjunction with the Atomic Energy Research Authority. Two new buildings had just been completed in 1956, one for radiological work and another for low temperature research, both of which were occupied by the Physics Division. Progress had also been made on the construction work for the new NPL Ship Hydrodynamics Laboratory at Feltham. The main fabric of this laboratory was expected to be completed early in 1957.

Building the Feltham Ship Tank, 1955.

Before the end of 1956, the civil service implemented the introduction of a five-day week (from a five and a half-day week) for non-industrial staff. This necessitated some changes in arrangements – particularly those made for parties who visited the Laboratory on Saturdays, and those of certain members of the industrial grades of staff, who were already accustomed to a five-day week and would be paid for working overtime on Saturday mornings.

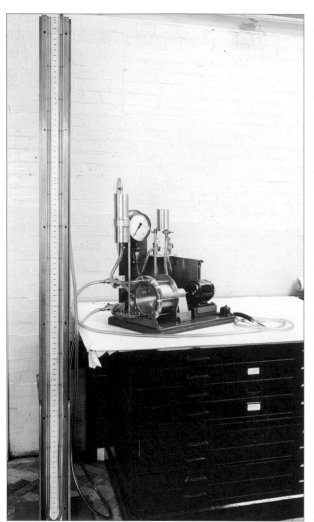

Apparatus for investigating the rate of solution of air from bubbles in water, 1954.

Expansion of the NPL

The programme for expansion began to take shape in the spring of 1957. By then, several of the divisions had their work scattered in various parts of the grounds and some were housed in a very unsuitable manner. The top priorities were a new library, lecture hall and canteen; these were followed by the need for various laboratories, workshops and offices. All major building requirements for the Aerodynamics Division were provided for by the Ministry of Supply. The buildings needed included a shock tube laboratory, a hypersonic wind tunnel and a general purpose atmospheric wind tunnel. The Mathematics and Metrology Divisions needed to be rehoused. The Physics Building was near completion and plans were made for the erection of a laboratory for the Light Division.

Yet concerns were voiced about the policy of the DSIR and, in particular, about not letting the quality and quantity of work done at the NPL become inferior to corresponding bodies in Germany and Canada. (Sutherland avoided making comparisons with the US Bureau of Standards because this created much controversy and also because the Bureau did much sponsored research.) A year later, in May 1958, the Executive Committee began to plan the second five-year plan for 1959-1963. The Executive Committee recommended to the Council for Scientific and Industrial Research that three of the present nine divisions be reorganised, as it believed this would introduce new flexibility and vitality throughout the NPL. The Metrology, Electricity and Physics Divisions were replaced by three new divisions: Standards, Applied Physics and Basic Physics.

The Standards Division, based on the old Metrology Division, was to be responsible for determining fundamental standards of mass, length, frequency, temperature and for units of electricity and magnetism. Its main objectives were the basic support of science and industry by the maintenance and improvement of certain important standards of measurements, particularly those of length and also those of mass and some simple derivatives such as density, load, pressure and hardness. It was also responsible for the improved determination of some physical quantities as well as more direct assistance to industry through research, development and an advisory service to meet requirements for increased accuracy for all these quantities. The division was subdivided into two main groups dealing with physical and engineering metrology.

The Applied Physics Division covered secondary standards, electrotechnics, acoustics, light, radiology and the Test House. Two new

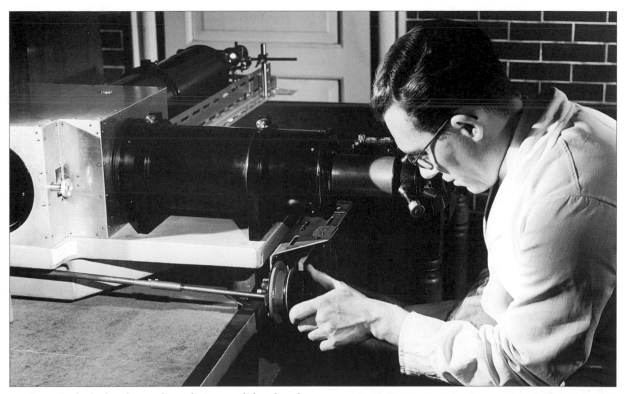

projects included radio-carbon dating and the development of a national centre for neutron-source standardisation. Apparatus was constructed to enable radio-carbon dating measurements to be carried out at the Laboratory. It was intended that a national service should be provided to meet the needs of archaeologists, botanists and geologists. Electrotechnics was a section of the former Electricity Division along with electrical standards and high voltage. The Light Division was also organised in three sections: radiometry and light standards; photometry and colorimetry; and optics. In addition there were two research units dealing with visual research and diffraction gratings and their applications. It was felt that this division should establish close relations with industry and that a considerable proportion of its work should be financially self-supporting. The Test House was formed to group together all the routine calibration and verification work of the Laboratory, to improve the efficiency of the services provided to industry while also allowing the other divisions to devote their resources to research work.

The Basic Physics Division was responsible for pioneering developments in non-nuclear physics which were also of potential importance to industry. The superintendent of the new Basic Physics Division, Dr

top *The Universal Camera Lens Interferometer, 1954.* **bottom** *Two types of balance for accurate measurement of high pressure, 1953.*

Apparatus for the measurement of pressure-volume-temperature relations of gases and gas mixtures, 1953.

J A Pople, took up his post on October 1st 1958. He proposed to begin work on the application of magnetic resonance to the study of the structure and properties of materials. The Mathematics Division was reorganised to take account of the change in circumstances in which the scientists worked. The new sections of this division consisted of Numerical Analysis and Table Making, High-Speed Computing Techniques, Applied Mathematics and General Computation.

Recommendations were also made by the Executive Committee for the separate divisions in the second five-year plan. The Standards Division was to expand considerably and would be encouraged to strengthen and concentrate its resources upon a limited number of areas of basic research of current importance. The Physics Division was to be allowed to recruit a number of staff with the necessary qualifications. It was thought that the Control Mechanism and Electronics Division was still below the desired size as proposed in 1953. It was also suggested that the Mathematics Division ought to move away from the design and construction of computers, to study the means of mechanising human faculties other than the ability to count. The importance of the contribution of the Light Division to industry was recognised and a small increase in staff was made.

Rolls Royce rotating bending fatigue machine for fatigue testing at high temperatures, 1953.

New buildings

By 1957, the Executive Committee urged that the erection of a building incorporating a first-class lecture hall, restaurant facilities and a library should be made without further delay. Once completed, this would allow the NPL to organise scientific gatherings appropriately and to replace the outmoded arrangements for midday meals for the staff. Equally urgent was the need for a new building for the Control Mechanism and Electronics (CME) Division.

During 1957, the rehousing of some sections in the Physics Division was completed. Ultrasonics was moved to Victoria House, which for many years had been the home of Temperature Measurement. The Smith Bridge, and its ancillary equipment for precise thermometry, was installed on the ground floor of the Physics Building. The calibration of high-grade thermometers and thermocouples was also undertaken in the Physics Building.

By April 1958, the reorganisation of the work of the Electricity, Metrology and Physics Divisions had taken place. The Review Committee of the Council for Scientific and Industrial Research emphasised the importance of increasing the impact of the work of the Laboratory on

137

Excavations in the High Voltage Laboratory, Electricity Division, showing the reinforced wall, 1958.

industry. The committee suggested this could be accomplished by firms seconding staff to the Laboratory to accelerate the industrial development of techniques and equipment which evolved from pioneering research in the Laboratory.

Industrial liaison service

The Laboratory Liaison Committee originally formed in 1945 was renamed the Lecture and Liaison Committee in 1957. More emphasis was laid on the promotion of scientific liaison between the divisions and subcommittees to deal with solid-state physics, fluid dynamics and mathematical methods. There were 37 meetings arranged in 1957 and speakers for 20 meetings came from members of the NPL staff. The industries in which large and small firms had been helped included manufacturing electrical and electronic equipment, precision instruments, aircraft, gas turbines, diesel engines, nuclear power plants, non-ferrous metals, chemicals, synthetic textile materials, telephones, plastics, motor cars, oil, food and control equipment.

In 1961, the Executive Committee reviewed its plans for fixed quinquennial periods. Under the scheme, plans had to be laid at least a year ahead of the quinquennium; but these inevitably became out of date within two years or so, and it became clear that a more flexible arrangement was needed. The Council for Scientific and Industrial Research recommended that the NPL revise its quinquennial proposal by reassessing its plans annually. This then made it possible to coordinate all future proposals over a five-year period without the fear that it would be impossible to make adjustments in later years.

The Executive Committee also reported in 1961 that additional staff were needed: to enable the Laboratory to play a proper role in such emerging fields as ultrahigh pressure and polymer physics, optical masers and autonomics; and to expand work in metallurgy, radiology, industrial aerodynamics, hydrodynamics and mathematics.

The NPL's search for a well-defined industrial role continued during the 1960s and early 1970s. There was much debate over whether the NPL should concentrate on consolidating its strengths or give more attention to the weak points in British research and development. In 1964, the Ministry of Technology was set up – this development will be discussed in *Chapter 16.*

CHAPTER 15

Computers at the NPL

One of the first attempts to produce a computing machine in Britain was undertaken by Charles Babbage in 1812, when he devised his Analytical and Difference Engines. Babbage's efforts were made possible due to the emergence of the new fields of thermodynamics and electromagnetism, together with their application to problems in industry. By the end of the nineteenth century, hand-operated calculating machines had become commonplace. The original meaning of the term "computer" was used to describe an individual who undertook computing (rather than the machine he or she used). Such human computers would "compute" various calculations for wages, actuarial tables, astronomical predictions and biological statistics. In the early part of the twentieth century, human calculators and human computers could be found working in such mathematical laboratories as Karl Pearson's Biometric Laboratory at University College London, E T Whittaker's mathematical laboratory at Edinburgh and at the Nautical Almanac Office (NAO).

Before the Second World War, there were three types of calculating machines in use in Britain: mechanical and electromechanical hand calculators; electromechanical punched-card machines, such as sorters and tabulators; and analogue devices, ranging from planimeters and integrators to differential analysers built during the 1930s at Cambridge and Manchester. From 1935 to 1945, the application of electronics to "automatic computers" generally referred to developing faster calculating equipment for specific problems. By the mid-1940s, there were several research groups in Britain, the United States and Germany who were interested in building large-scale calculating machines for military purposes.

During the Second World War, various computational problems

Brunsviga hand calculator.

emerged, including: computation of trajectories of missiles (ballistics); flight simulation; code deciphering; and radio signal processing. Large-scale calculations were also needed for the computation of astronomical tables for purposes of navigation (this was the responsibility of the Nautical Almanac Office in the Admiralty, but work had increased during the war due to the collapse of international co-operation). The armed services expanded their computing capacity when the External Ballistics Board of the Ministry of Supply took over the Cambridge Mathematical Laboratory. To meet the increasing computational demands, an Admiralty Computing Service was established in 1943. The increased need for fast computing brought about the construction of storage computing machines during the Second World War. The first large-scale use of thermionic valves (a binary on-off information storage device) for digital computation was introduced during the war. (A valve is an evacuated glass tube in which some electrodes are made to control the flow of electrons – the electron being produced by heating a cathode electrode.)

A special purpose all-electronic deciphering computer named COLOSSUS was developed by Tommy Flowers and M H A Newman at the Post Office Research Station for the government Code and Cipher School at Bletchley Park in Buckinghamshire. The machine, which was assembled at the Post Office Research Station at Dollis Hill, London, was able to decipher the Germans' Enigma code. COLOSSUS contained electronics for counting, making comparisons, performing simple

COLOSSUS

COUNTERS

FIG. 4

binary arithmetic and doing logical operations. The work of a number of mathematicians, including that of Alan Turing, made the decoding of large number of messages practical.

COLOSSUS code-cracking machine at Bletchley Park, 1943.

A few of the early stored computers were electromechanical, based on devices called relays. A relay is a switch that can be opened or closed automatically by appropriate electrical signals. The activating mechanism is an electromagnet which can "pull" the switch contacts together. Simon Lavington has noted that relays were a comparatively cheap way of implementing computing and control equipment, though they were unsuitable for use in constructing realistic storage units.[10] The main disadvantages for their use in processing data were their slowness of operation and relative unreliability (due to constant wear and susceptibility to dust). A relay took a few milliseconds (thousandths of a second) to "switch" whereas a thermionic valve circuit would switch in less than a microsecond (less than one millionth of a second). While electrical relays made binary computation practical, the remaining mechanical components placed a physical limit on the speed of computation.

In 1946, there were two ways of storing information for use in automatic computers. The first involved passing acoustic waves down a column, while the second method stored spots of charge on the inside of a cathode-ray tube. The Moore College of Engineering at the University of Pennsylvania developed the acoustic line using a five-foot column of mercury and pulse rates of a megacycle. With the support of the US

left *Alan Turing (by courtesy of the National Portrait Gallery). London.* **right** *E T (Charles) Goodwin.*

Army's technical liaison, it developed the first all-electronic computer, the Electronic Numerical Integrator and Automatic Calculator (ENIAC), which came on line in 1946. In Britain, F C Williams developed the cathode-ray tube for computers. From 1948 to 1955, most computers used thermionic valves in their processors. In contrast, modern electronic components control the flow of charged particles inside a solid piece of semiconducting material – hence the term "solid-state circuits".

The first major innovation in solid-state components occurred in 1947, when William Shockley devised the transistor at Bell Telephone Laboratories in Murray Hill, New Jersey. By the mid-1950s, transistors were reliable and cheap enough to replace valves. The advantages of using transistors were the reduction in physical size and in power control, but it was not until the mid-1960s when valves became obsolete because they became more expensive than transistors.

The NPL's central mathematical station

In March 1943, the director of the NPL, Charles Darwin, remarked at the Advisory Council meeting of the DSIR that he was of the opinion that a Mathematics Department should be established at the NPL which would facilitate computation and assist in the statistical design of quality control at the NPL. The DSIR recommended that an interdepartmental

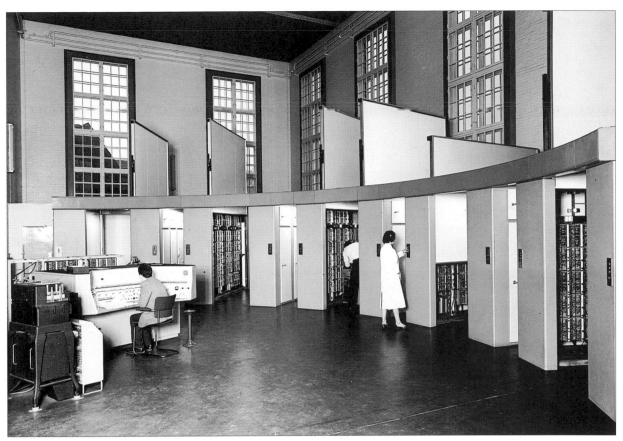

technical committee be set up to determine if a central mathematics station should indeed be established. The recommendation was accepted by the Advisory Council and the post of superintendent was offered to John Womersley of the Ministry of Supply Advisory Service on Statistical Methods.

ACE computer was used to develop sophisticated mathematical techniques for solving problems arising in the scientific divisions of NPL.

The official research programme for the new division in 1944 included the investigation of the "possible adaptation of automatic telephone equipment to scientific computing" and the development of an electronic counting device suitable for rapid computing. In setting up the Mathematics Division, Womersley was able to recruit wartime colleagues from the Ministry of Supply and some staff from the Admiralty Computing Services. Womersley's division replaced the Computing Services of the Admiralty. By October 1945, the division was housed in Teddington Hall and Cromer House, which were on the perimeters of the NPL. The Mathematics Division had set up sections for Desk Computing, Statistics, Punched-Cards, Differential Analysers and Electronics.

Alan Turing and ACE
Alan Turing played a vital role in the use and development of modern computers through his work on Pilot ACE and the ACE machines in the late 1940s. Turing's early research, first at Cambridge and then at

J H (Jim) Wilkinson.

Princeton, had been in mathematical logic, and this had led him to introduce the concept of "computable numbers" (and what became known later as "Turing Machines"). His war work at Bletchley Park and at the Foreign Office, which brought him into contact with digital electronics, provided him with knowledge of pulse techniques. It was this that led to his interest in the construction of an electronic computer. One of the central features of Turing's computing machines was the idea of the self-programming computer. The stored programme would enable the computer to modify its instructions and thus control the flow of computation in response to the results being generated.

Turing was not happy working under Womersley, nor did he have any high regard for Womersley's managerial skills. As far as Turing was concerned, the really important skill a superintendent ought to possess was the capacity for rational scientific argument. Although Womersley was a man of some dynamism and vision, he was not trained as a scientist. It transpired that Womersley's lengthy and expensive tour of the United States earlier in 1945 (see *Chapter 12*) had been a technical failure, since he had lacked the expertise to make a detailed analysis of what he had been allowed to see.

Nevertheless, Turing threw himself into the work of planning the logical design of an Automatic Computing Engine (ACE) with enthusiasm. Moreover, he reportedly enjoyed the alternation of abstract questions of design against practical engineering. It was Womersley who suggested the name "Automatic Computing Engine" (ACE) in honour of Charles Babbage's Analytical Engine, with which it had striking similarities. ACE was intended to be both faster and more complete than the American ENIAC, and was estimated by the DSIR to cost somewhere between £100,000 and £115,000. Turing went on to devise a universal procedure for reading the instruction of any Turing machine at the beginning of the tape. His machine contained the archetype of the stored-programme computers because the same tape could contain both instructions and data.

By November 1946, sufficient advances had been made for news of this venture to be broadcast on the BBC. As director of the NPL, Darwin remarked on the radio that "the project has been picturesquely called the Electronic Brain". In keeping with Turing's ability as an Olympic-class long-distance runner, one of the evening papers referred to his ACE machine as an "Electronic Athlete".

A decision was made quite early not to set up a hardware section at the NPL, but to subcontract this side of the work to other governmental departments – preferably where there had been previous experience

DEUCE installed in the former four-foot wind tunnel, 1956.

with pulse techniques. Jim Wilkinson recalled later that he considered this decision to be deplorable at the time. In January 1947, the American mathematician Harry Huskey came to Teddington for one year to work on the ACE project. Since the NPL had decided not to be responsible for hardware, Huskey suggested to Womersley that the group build a prototype, which was based on Turing's version V. The machine was known as the "Test Assembly".

Wilkinson, who was involved in the Test Assembly project, thought, in retrospect, that it was an impractical objective for two reasons. Firstly, Huskey was halfway through his year when the construction of the Test Assembly began, and most of the members of the ACE section did not have the relevant background experience and were just "learning on the job". Another difficulty for most people working in the electronics area in the United Kingdom at this time was the problem of supplies. By the late summer, Darwin had decided that the mathematicians did not know enough about electronics to build a computer and in 1947 the policy of trying to get the computer built outside was finally abandoned. It was then decided that the Radio Division should become involved.

By the early part of 1949, work had begun again on the Pilot ACE which was again based on Turing's version V. The first half of the machine was assembled rapidly, but by the end of the year progress had become slower. On May 10th 1950, the ACE team was working on all the basic pulse circuits, the control unit, one long delay line and a short delay line fitted with an additive and a subtractive unit. It devised a very elementary programme consisting of a few instructions. The programme worked and the computer was running. The programme was christened "Successive Digits"; it was used throughout the life of Pilot ACE and DEUCE and was affectionately known as "Suck Digs".

Now that it had a computer that worked, the division found itself under pressure to mount a demonstration for the press. In the event, the Pilot ACE worked virtually perfectly for the whole three days that it was set up for the press, though it did not attain this level of performance for several months after the first successful run. At this time the Pilot ACE was the only computer in a British government department. During 1953-4, the ACE machine was used for the calculation of critical flutter speeds and stress analysis computation for aircraft firms. Additionally, a large amount of work was done for the Ministry of Supply and for some members of the Royal Aircraft Establishment, to solve problems on the large amount of data from the flight trials of the Comet. In collaboration with the Atomic Energy Research Establishment, a punched card method was established for the analysis of spectrum lines. Data collected by the British Boot, Shoe and Allied Trades Research Association on women's feet was being analysed to improve the available range of fittings. Despite outside interest, the defence ministries and the aircraft industry were the two groups which accounted for the greater part of the division's paid work.

Research connected with the ACE had mostly been concerned with the production of programmes for problems in linear algebra, including the solution of linear equations, evaluation of determinants, inversion of matrices and the calculation of their latent roots. The number of problems coming down from the division had steadily increased. The main areas using the services of ACE were Aerodynamics, Metrology and the Physics Divisions. The largest and one of the most difficult pieces of computing to be tackled by the division in 1953 was connected with Edward Bullard's theory of the origin of the earth's magnetic field. Other uses of the ACE machine came from the National Coal Board, which wanted to analyse the warning system used in coal mines, and the English Electric Company which produced a programme for computing train time-tables.

During the period when the Pilot ACE was being built, the English Electric Company became interested in electronic computers. A small group from the company joined the ACE section in 1952 and stayed until 1955. This group helped to build a computer marketed under the name DEUCE (Digital Electronic Universal Computing Engine) which was installed in the former four-foot wind tunnel at the NPL. The first

DEUCE was completed in the workshop of the English Electric Nelson Research Laboratories in Staffordshire.

By 1955, a section of the Pay As You Earn (PAYE) Tax Tables was computed on the Pilot ACE on the evening of Budget day. The work was organised by a member of the English Electric Company staff working in the Mathematics Division. An important problem for the Admiralty concerned the analysis of stresses set up in the steam catapult retardation structure in *HMS Ark Royal*; this involved the ACE in the solution of more than 20 simultaneous non-linear differential equations with discontinuous coefficients.

A second ACE derivative was the MOSAIC (Ministry of Supply Automatic Computer) which was constructed under the direction of A W M Coombs at the Post Office Research Station in Dollis Hill. This computer was developed for the analysis of radar data and reflected the strong emphasis on national defence. Throughout 1955, the DEUCE had, on average, at least one visitor per day and 80 hours of demonstration were given. The Pilot ACE was dismantled in June 1955 and put on exhibition at the Science Museum. Three years later, in January 1958, the next ACE machine was completed and was expected to be fully operational by the summer. The computational work for the Royal Aircraft Establishment came to an end in 1955, when it acquired its second DEUCE. By 1958, most of the staff at the NPL had experience of using DEUCE. A computer programme was completed for the study of name-indexing at the Ministry of Pensions and National Insurance in 1959.

Steady progress throughout the 1950s in the Autonomics Division, led to new areas of information processing and automatic control by the early 1960s. One of the main functions of computers in the Autonomics Division was to pursue aspects of fundamental research associated with various industrial requirements of very high-speed computers as well as the efficient retrieval of scientific information in very large libraries. In April 1963 the Autonomics Division moved into its specially-designed new building.

Three years after the Ministry of Technology was established in 1964, the Autonomics Division was renamed the Division of Computer Science. The division was also responsible for the technical management of the Ministry of Technology's Advanced Computer Technology Project (ACTP). The object of ACTP was to extend by cost-share contracts with industry the computer technology available in Britain. There was a widespread range of work which included studies of human visual perception and neural mechanisms. These and other biological studies could benefit by contact with information technology and could also occasionally contribute to engineering knowledge.

A crucial factor in the growth of computer usage was the increasing availability, suitability and cost of communication facilities. By the late 1960s, many organisations such as banks, airlines and public utilities were using large central multi-access computers. These organisations set up their own data networks by hiring private lines. The NPL was setting up its own network so that it could provide a highly flexible means of communicating digital information between all parts of the Laboratory.

The British computing industry, however, was unable to capture a substantial share of either the domestic or international market, and was slowly squeezed out by American competition. The reason for the subsequent American near-monopoly in the international computer market from the 1950s was due mainly to US government sponsorship of military and civilian projects for which large sums were made available for investment. Meanwhile in Britain the industry was virtually ignored. By 1965, customers in America could choose from among more than 100 models offered by over 20 manufacturers; an additional 100 models were available from over 25 companies worldwide. The advent of the minicomputer around 1970 and of the microcomputer a decade later, brought similar spurts of growth to the industry.

CHAPTER 16

The Ministry of Technology

British industry in general should be based on advanced technology so that it may keep ahead of its main competitors . . . (and) the traditional craft industries should no longer continue to be craftsman-based but should employ technologists with a more flexible outlook, who will need to keep a continuous watch for new ideas worth applying.

Lord Hailsham, Minster of Science, November 1960.

In the early 1960s, the Executive Committee and the deputy director, J V Dunworth, felt that much of the routine work at the NPL ought no longer be the main function of a modern laboratory. It considered it increasingly unrealistic for a single institution to undertake a variety of activities ranging from the testing of thermometers to the use of computers. The 1960s heralded the rapid growth of what came to be known as "big science" which included quantum physics, atomic energy, molecular science, modern computers and weapons technologies. Additional staff were needed to enable the Laboratory to play a proper role in such new fields as ultra-high pressure and polymer physics, optical masers – now more commonly called lasers – and autonomics as well as to expand work in metallurgy, radiology, industrial aerodynamics, hydrodynamics and mathematics. To make room for new areas, certain items were dropped from the programme. For example, the work on high-voltage phenomena ended in 1961 to create new posts for investigations on optical masers and radiology.

New buildings were built to house the Basic Physics and Autonomics Divisions together with a metal-working shop for metallurgy. Recommendations were made that the Administration, Light, Mathematics and Standard Divisions be re-housed during 1967. A new circulatory

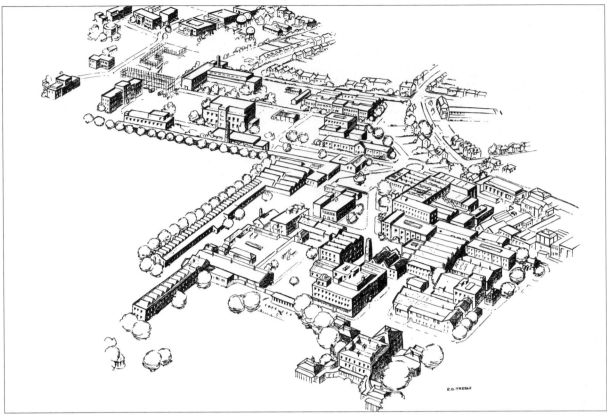

NPL site, 1960.

water channel, recently approved for installation at Feltham, was to provide for potentially important studies on model ships which could not be undertaken with the existing equipment. In the Metallurgy Division, work was done with the electron microscope which made an important contribution to the fundamental study of the role of dislocation in age hardening in fatigue and creep. The Radiology Section of the Applied Physics Division needed to expand to accommodate its growing responsibility for standards work in the nuclear power field and for determining ionising radiation standards in the medical field. Recommendations were also made for a more modern and more powerful computer for the Mathematics Division. Nevertheless, the new programme of advanced computer research and development launched by the DSIR in 1961 was seen to be of "outstanding importance for industry". The DSIR with the NPL aimed to increase research in Britain on new components and techniques for future computers.

At the end of 1961, it was agreed that the traditional and routine thermometer testing should be transferred to the British Standards Institution (BSI). The transfer aroused much opposition within the industrial sector which was convinced that the loss of the NPL mark on thermometers would hinder British competition in foreign markets. After much heated debate, the transfer took place in April 1963. Activities in the NPL Test House decreased by 30 per cent and it was absorbed into the Standards

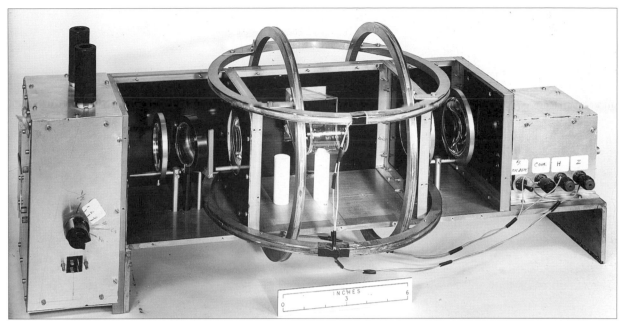

Division in 1965. An important part of the work of the Laboratory remained, nonetheless, the setting and maintenance of standards of measurement. At the General Conference of Weights and Measures in 1960, the wavelength of light was adopted as the fundamental standard of length. The metre was redefined in terms of a particular number of wavelengths of light emitted by a krypton-86 lamp, and the yard defined as a specific fraction of the metre

During this time, the DSIR had been considering ways of stimulating technological progress. It had encouraged its research associations to develop its Information and Liaison Service to make results available to industry. It had also begun to place development contracts in industry, and the emergent area of computers was one in which the DSIR wished to improve co-ordination in industry and government laboratories. Though there were signs of an increasing response from industry, progress had been slow. The DSIR had wanted to see more rapid advances in machine-tool development and more formal arrangements were made whereby representatives of the industry selected machine-tool users, and the DSIR co-operated in an attempt to identify development projects which required government support. It was also thought that the field of engineering materials was one from which great technological and economical advances would flow.

The Aerodynamics Division focused its attention on hypersonic flow, including low-density flow, which was concerned with the aero-dynamics of flights at speeds more than five times that of sound. Research related to transonic and supersonic speeds centred on the aerodynamic design of aircraft with highly swept wings. The Ship Division studied hydrodynamic problems which affected the performance of ships, principally through experiments with models.

Gas-cell frequency standard, 1962. Optical pumping of caesium or rubidium atoms in a gas-cell was used as an atomic frequency standard yielding stabilities of the order of one part in 10^{10} per year.

151

The one metre interference comparator for measuring length bars directly in light waves, 1963.

New sub-divisions

In the early 1960s, new subsections were created for the NPL's major divisions. In 1961, the Applied Physics Division was organised into five sections including Radiology, Acoustics, Electrotechnics, the Test House and High Voltage. The Light Division came of age in 1961, 21 years after it was formed into a division by the union of the Optics and Photometry Departments. The division comprised three main sections consisting of Optics, Radiation and Standards, and also Applied Photometry and Colorimetry.

The Mathematics Division was divided into three main groups. The Numerical Methods Group worked in the broad fields of numerical analysis and high speed computing techniques and also prepared mathematical tables. The Applied Mathematics Group did research into the application of high speed computers while the General Computing Group assisted the research groups.

The Metallurgy Division was organised in six sections dealing with Metal Physics, X-ray Analysis, Mechanical Properties, Iron Alloys, Non-ferrous Metals and Alloys and also Chemistry. Approximately two-thirds of the work in this division consisted of fundamental investigations on subjects relevant to problems of the metal-producing and metal-using industry. The work of the Standards Division comprised three groups: Physical, Electrical and Mechanical. All physical measurements are based on a number of fundamental, independent units such as mass, length, time and electric current. Until the 1950s, these were all based on either material or astronomical standards. With the expansion and growth of science in the 1960s, these base units were progressively being redefined in terms of atomic properties. Mass has yet to be redefined in atomic terms. Thus, not only could the wavelength of spectrum lines be compared more accurately than graduated scales, but also frequencies of atomic transitions could be compared more accurately than celestial events.

In addition to providing reliable measurements for a very wide range of quantities in mechanics, electromagnetics and temperature, by the 1960s, accurate measurements also had to be made for stabilised electromagnetic frequencies and wavelengths; gravitational acceleration and the gravitational constant; the gyromagnetic ratio of the proton; the quantum of magnetism and the charge-to-mass ratios of the proton and the electron. By 1963, the DSIR had to admit that the distribution of funding between basic research, applied research, development and information and the advisory services was problematic due to the competition for scarce resources. The outcome was that the NPL was finding it difficult to get the support necessary to sustain a significant rate of growth. Despite the continuing development of basic research in the emergent fields of ultra-high pressure and polymer physics, optical masers and autonomics, the DSIR was not convinced that the NPL needed additional staff for those areas.

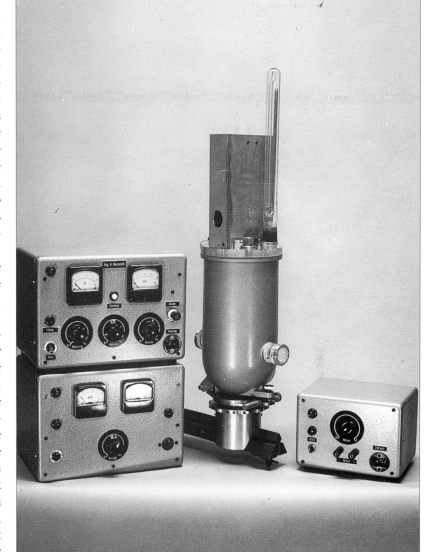

Krypton lamp cryostat modified for use with electrodeless lamps. The very high frequency oscillator is mounted on the cryostat cover, 1959.

The Trend Report

It was not only the DSIR that was unsympathetic to the NPL's new orientation, industry was also unwilling to undertake certain research ventures. Though the Laboratory was quite academic in character, most of the work of the DSIR research stations was often too basic to be of interest

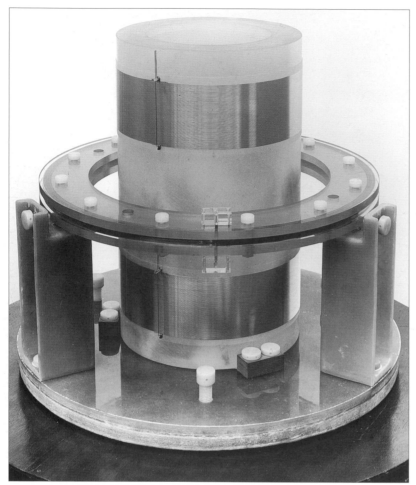

Campbell standard of mutual inductance completed at the NPL in 1960 and used for the determination of the Ohm, 1960.

to the practical businessman. A report on the government's role in promoting research and development, set up by the Conservative Party's Advisory Committee on Policy, claimed that there was a danger the DSIR's research stations might become quiet scientific backwaters remote from the stimulus of contact with wider fields of research, and the daily problems of industry.

In 1962, a Treasury committee, under Sir Burke Trend, was set up to investigate the whole field of civil sciences. A year later when Harold Wilson spoke of the "white heat of technology", he stressed the need for research by means of "new and larger government organisations … for applying science on a really massive scale in civil industry". Wilson's political overtones were, however, unwelcomed by many in the Conservative Party. The Trend Report appeared in October 1963 and had a cool reception. It emphasised that new problems had been created due to the acceleration and rate of expansion of scientific activity since the Second World War, the speed of technological developments, and the growth of international co-operation in scientific research.

The report proposed the disbanding of the DSIR and its replacement by a number of research councils. In addition, it was suggested that an industrial research and development authority (IRDA) should be set up. Considerable discussions arose as to whether the NPL should become a part of the proposed scientific research council of the IRDA. At this time, the director of the NPL, Sir Gordon Sutherland, moved to Cambridge to become the master of Emmanuel College.

When J V Dunworth was appointed director in 1964, this marked the beginning of a new style of appointments. All previous directors, including Glazebrook, Petavel, Darwin and Sutherland, had been fellows of the Royal Society. While all were distinguished academically, they had extremely limited experience of industry. Sutherland wanted to promote a more academically-inclined environment at the NPL by forging closer links with other universities through extra-mural research contracts, and curtailing work that industry was capable of

J V Dunworth.

undertaking itself. He was also responsible for helping to create the Division of Basic Physics which had more to do with academic research, but its use for industry was limited. For Sutherland, the functions of the NPL were, first and foremost, to establish, maintain and improve standards of physical measurement, and second, to encourage, assist, and where necessary, to pioneer the application of physics in industry. The promotion of pure research, without much consideration of industrial application, created an élitist environment within the NPL. The elitism prompted scientists in other laboratories to refer to the NPL as the "University of Teddington".

In the winter of 1964, the government announced the formation of the Department of Education and Science under Quentin Hogg (as Lord Hailsham became on his return to the Commons). At the same time, the main proposals of the Trend Report were to be implemented and the DSIR was to be dissolved and replaced by three new research councils. With the return of the Labour government in October 1964, a Ministry of Technology was established. It was then decided that the NPL should amalgamate with the National Chemical Laboratory (NCL)

Chemical Research Laboratory, 1957.

whose facilities adjoined those of the NPL at Teddington. The amalgamated laboratories became part of the new ministry. The ministry became the sponsoring department within the government for computers, electronics, mechanical and electrical engineering, machine tools and telecommunication industries. Upon taking up the directorship, Dunworth advocated the idea that the NPL should be the National Standards Laboratory. This idea was greatly facilitated by the spread of scientific disciplines resulting from the merger between the NPL and the NCL in 1965.

The ministry was also responsible for the United Kingdom Atomic Energy Authority, which was first set up in 1954 as an independent agency of the government to undertake research and development in the production of atomic energy. Under the Ministry of Technology, the most fundamental change was the abolition of the Royal Society's Executive Committee – a body that had been a part of the NPL's organisation for 65 years. The NPL had now become a government institution in every sense and there its formal constitutional links with the scientific community no longer existed.

The production of interference gratings for spectroscopy. A laser beam is divided and then recombined to generate a very fine pattern of interference fringes which are then recorded in a photosensitive material to form the grooves of a grating.

The amalgamation of the NPL and the NCL

A year later in November 1965, an agreement was made between the Royal Society and the Ministry of Technology for the future management of the policy of the NPL. It was decided that in the future the president and council of the Royal Society would be associated with the Ministry of Technology in the management of scientific policy at the NPL. A new advisory body, the Advisory Committee for Research on Measurements and Standards, was formed with strong Royal Society

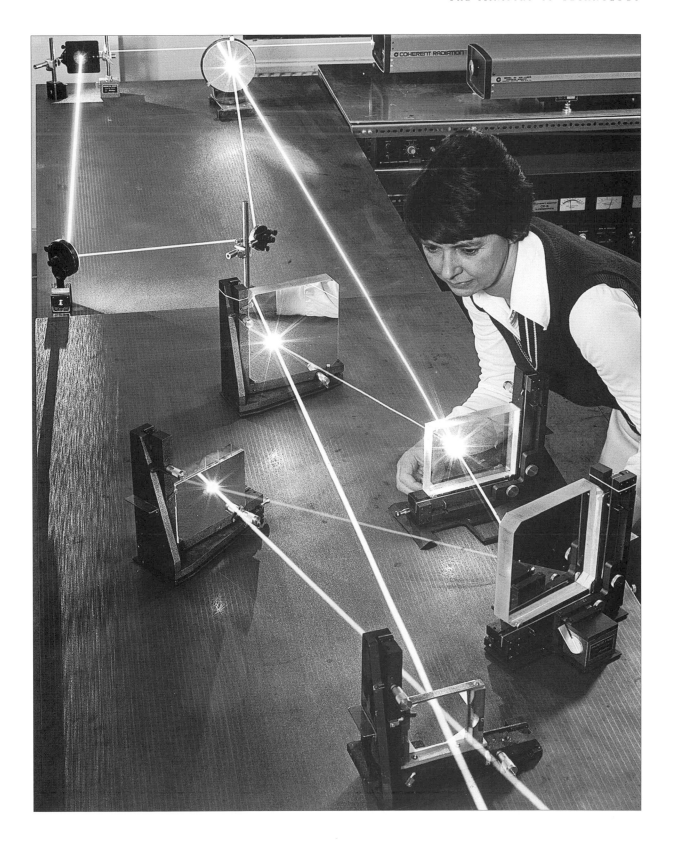

Hydrogen maser. On the shelf may be seen a quartz storage bulb, a focusing magnet and an early type of discharge tube, 1967.

representation under the chairmanship of Professor Nicholas Kurti. This committee monitored and reviewed all the measurement work of NPL, reporting annually to ministers, for the next six years until the new Requirements Board system was in place (see *Chapter 17*).

Following the amalgamation of the NPL and the NCL, plans were made to organise the combined Laboratories into three groups consisting of Measurement, Material and a Third Group. Two years later, the Third Group was renamed The Engineering Sciences Group. Following these changes, the scientific staff represented at the NPL included physicists, chemists, mathematicians and metallurgists, as well as engineers of aerodynamics, mechanics, electricity and marine science.

The Measurement Group

Within the Measurement Group there were five specialised divisions: Quantum Metrology, Electrical Science, Optical Metrology, Radiation Science and the Metrology Centre. The Division of Quantum Metrology reflected the modern trend to establish standards in terms of atomic phenomena and comprised three groups: Quantum Electronics, Quantitative Spectroscopy and Thermodynamics. Quantum Electronics concentrated on the establishment of frequency standards; the work

of Quantitative Spectroscopy was concerned principally with the measurement of radiant energy; and Thermodynamics established methods of measuring very low and very high temperatures. This division replaced the Standards Division. Its main purpose remained the maintenance and development of fundamental standards and methods of measurement in physics and engineering.

Mekometre. An electro-optic long distance measuring instrument designed for mechanical and civil engineering or general survey work, 1967.

While the standard of length was formerly determined by the separation of two lines on a metal bar, it was now measured by a particular wavelength emitted by atoms of krypton-86. The outstanding advantage of atomic quantum phenomena as standards is that they are the same whenever they are measured and a standard established in one laboratory could be reproduced with assurance elsewhere. The realisation of programmes on these lines required accurate knowledge of the fundamental constants of atomic physics. This division was devoted to the study of the primary standards, and to the basic science required to improve the ways in which these primary standards together with the related physical constants were determined and maintained. Members of this division had the task of applying ideas and the method of quantum physics to the improvement of standards and methods of measurement in physics and engineering.

The Division of Electrical Science was newly formed on November 1st 1967. This division maintained the basic electrical standards and enabled the Laboratory to provide specialist services in the fields of electrical measurement and radio frequencies, microwave and infra-red frequencies. It was also concerned with the use of electromagnetic techniques of measurement of non-electrical quantities. The most important commercial electrical measurement was that of power, for on it depended the measurement of energy that was bought and sold for millions of pounds annually.

The Division of Optical Metrology promoted the use of optical methods of measurement in all appropriate fields and applied optical principles to the development of instruments and of measuring techniques applicable in industry. The division also had responsibility for the measurement of time – the realisation of the SI Unit, the second. This work included the development of atomic time, based on Essen's earlier pioneering work with the caesium clock. The advent of the laser was greatly increasing the accuracy and applicability of optical methods in the measurement of the size and shape of engineering components. NPL's pioneering work on diffraction gratings for metrology as well as spectroscopy was also pursued in this division

The Division of Radiation Science was devoted to the development of methods of measurement and to the establishment of standards for ionising radiation and for radioactivity. The need for such measurement stemmed largely from the requirements of hospital physicists and from the legislation and codes of practice which had been introduced to ensure the safety of workers and the general public, particularly in relation to the practice of radiation therapy.

The Division of Quantum Metrology added a Metrology Centre on December 1st 1966 to co-ordinate the Laboratory's calibration and advisory services to industry in the better-established technologies. It also acted as a focus for collaboration with the British Calibration Service (BCS) of the Ministry of Technology, the British Standards Institution (BSI) and various international standards organisations. The centre was originally based on the engineering group of the Standards Division. Just over a year after the centre had been set up, the NPL Test House and the Colorimetry and Vision Group of the Quantum Metrology Division was transferred to the centre. The Metrology Centre was the group's main focus for industrial enquires. The services it offered to industry dealt with calibration and information. The calibration service ranged from the most precise measurements to relatively routine calibrations. Most of the latter were by now being transferred to industrial laboratories under the growing British Calibration Service scheme, though a good variety of special test work such as reflectometry, routine calibration of instruments including certain types of viscometers and pyrometers was also undertaken. In addition to testing certain types of measurement equipment, the Metrology Centre assessed the advantages and disadvantages of new instrument designs.

HD2 an experimental hovercraft on Southampton Water, 1967.

The Engineering Sciences Group

The Engineering Sciences Group, which was the largest of the three groups, served the technologies associated with air and sea transport and with computer usage. The activities of this group were directed to a number of distinct industries through the basic sciences supporting fluid dynamics, mathematics and computer sciences. Fluid dynamics dealt with the aerodynamics and hydrodynamics, both aeronautical and industrial. The work on aeronautical aerodynamics was largely related to the study of flow over swept wings, while industrial applications included the study of the behaviour of wind on suspension bridges and on large elastic structures such as towers and power station chimneys. Its work also influenced the design of civil aircraft including helicopters. The Acoustics Section was part of the Aerodynamics Division and dealt with the study of physical and auditory phenomena. Contacts with industry, government departments and standardising organisations played an important role in the section's work on aircraft, traffic and industrial noise as well as the transmission and absorption of sounds by building materials. The Ship Division undertook diverse hydrodynamic studies for ship-owners and builders. It had become increasingly concerned with high-speed craft (including the Hovercraft) and general problems with marine technology. The Hovercraft Unit, at Hythe on Southampton Water, carried out research on applications of the air cushion principle, mainly to marine hovercraft and also to

161

industrial lifting and sealing systems.

The Division of Numerical and Applied Mathematics, the Division of Computer Science and the Central Computer Unit were all concerned with the development of new mathematical methods and new software for computers. They also undertook work on the creation of new concepts for the interaction between users and computers, and the establishment of new types of networks for data processing and communication, and, of particular importance was Donald Davies' work on packet-switching.

Networks and packet-switching

One of the first forms of global telecommunication involved voice telephony from the work of Alexander Graham Bell in 1876. This was based on circuit-switching, which happens when an electrical circuit is established between two subscribers. Davies, who was superintendent of the Division of Computer Science in 1966, wanted a fast message-switching service (which allows messages to be stored briefly at the nodes in a computer network) where long messages would be automatically split into chunks and sent separately, so that they could be interleaved with chunks of other messages. The chunks were called packets and the technique became known as "packet-switching". Two years earlier in 1964, Paul Baran, of the RAND Corporation, had worked out the principles of packet-switching for a military communication network. In 1967, work was undertaken on packet-switching by Larry Roberts, at the Advanced Research Projects Agency (ARPA) of the US Department of Defense. The first practical networks using packet-switching were the ARPANET which evolved into the Internet and the NPL local network. The packet-switching technique formed the basis of the worldwide complex of computer communication systems today.

The Materials Group

The Materials Group was reorganised in 1967 into four divisions, including Chemical Standards, Inorganic and Metallic Structure, Materials Application and Molecular Science. The Division of Chemical Standards provided accurate thermodynamic data on pure chemical compounds or mixtures for the chemical design engineer. Its chief aim was the systematic measurement of physiochemical, thermodynamic and spectroscopic properties of substances that were important in technology and science. The data were needed by chemists, metallurgists and chemical engineers. In the formulation of the division's research programme, substances for study and properties for measurement were chosen on the advice given by the chemical industry. One important thermodynamic property was heat capacity. Molecular spectroscopy was an important part of the division's activities for measuring heat capacity, and recording spectrometers were able to cover the ultraviolet, infra-red and far infra-red regions. These spectrometers were used to calculate thermodynamic properties by the method of statistical mechanics.

The object of the Inorganic and Metallic Structure (IMS) Division was the study of the relationship between the microstructure and the properties of all inorganic materials which included metals, glasses, multiphase aggregates and artificially produced minerals. A fundamental understanding of the mechanical properties of materials required a concentrated study of defects on an atomic scale and instruments such as transmission electron microscopes were used to achieve this aim. This division embodied the whole of the Inorganic Unit and the former Metallurgy Division which had been concerned with the phase structure and defect structure of metals.

The Division of Materials Application was a new division established from part of the former Metallurgy Division. Its work aimed at understanding and solving those problems that prevented or inhibited the exploitation by industry of the various properties of both metallic and non-metallic materials. This enabled new technologies to be created and existing processes made more efficient and economic. The work undertaken by this division fell into two categories. The first was a study of the relation between the mechanical properties of industrial materials and their working condition; the second examined the effect of the chemical environment, and of high or low temperatures on the serviceability of materials.

A Division of Molecular Science was created on April 1st 1965, when the Organic and Inorganic Sections of the NCL were merged with the former Basic Physics Division of the NPL. The purpose of the new division was to conduct research on the synthesis and properties of new materials and to develop techniques and instruments that would lead to advances in the science of materials. It was concerned with the detailed study of structure and coupling in relatively complex molecules, polymers, molecular crystals and glasses. Advances in material science were seen to be inseparable from the development of new techniques of synthesis and evaluation. Thus, a major aim of the work was to pioneer the instrumentation for advanced methods of chemical synthesis and molecular spectroscopy. The major section on individual molecular properties was that of magnetic resonance. Magnetic resonance spectroscopy comprised an important part of the research, both in its application to the work in the division (e.g. polymers, free radical and paradigmatic centres) and also in the development of refined techniques in electron spin and nuclear magnetic resonance.

The resulting division was quite large which led to a regrouping into three sections concerned respectively with molecular science, inorganic material and advanced instrumentation. The Advanced Instrumentation Unit (AIU) was set up in April 1966 to create completely new instruments and devices. The majority of its personnel had worked together as the Infrared Spectroscopy Group in the Division of Molecular Science. The main focus in AIU was the development of submillimetre wave techniques and their applications in spectroscopy, metrology and communications. Some of the greatest achievements in this division,

163

were probably those of the AIU, including, in particular, Gebbie's world class work on Fourier transform spectroscopy which still has an impact on spectroscopy today.

The Royal Society, which continued to express an interest in the NPL, set up an ad hoc committee in June 1968 to discuss the future of the Laboratory with the Ministry of Technology. An agreement was reached that called for links between the NPL and the Royal Society to be re-established in the shape of a National Physical Laboratory Advisory Board. When the Conservative government replaced Labour in 1970, the Ministry of Technology was disbanded and the NPL was transferred to the Department of Trade and Industry (DTI). Given the advances and changes that the NPL had been undergoing throughout the 1960s, Russell Moseley has suggested that the Labour government would have taken a similar route probably through the creation of a British Research and Development Corporation which Labour had proposed in the green paper of 1970.[12]

CHAPTER 17

The Department of Trade and Industry

When the Department of Trade and Industry (DTI) took over the management of the NPL in 1971, it was keen to reduce the number of civil servants. The Laboratory achieved this by privatising certain services and by following the Rothschild Report of 1971, which advocated the "customer-contractor" principle as a framework for government research and development. The House of Commons Select Committee on Science and Technology cautioned, however, that this principle was "not necessarily the universal answer to the reorganisation of government research and development". Another outcome of the Rothschild Report was the formation of a series of research requirements boards in 1972. Dr I Maddock, who was then the DTI's chief scientist, hoped that the requirements boards, which were to act as "proxy customers", would produce a rare opportunity for open, public discussions concerning the government's industrial research establishment. The requirements boards were viewed as necessary by various scientists and superintendents at the NPL, as they made scientists more accountable and aware of how their work impinged on the public.

Eight research requirements boards were established, all intended to function as proxy customers representing both industry and government. Members of the requirements boards consisted of academics and industrialists. The NPL undertook work for all boards except those dealing with mechanical engineering and machine tools. The director, J V Dunworth, emphasised to the Select Committee on Science and Technology that most of the work at the NPL would continue to be for the government and that direct contract work for industry was "merely a spin-off". In June 1985 the requirements boards were reorganised into advisory committees, each aligned with the DTI's industrial sponsorship divisions.

Bushy House, North front, 1974.

Temporary casualties of the requirements boards were the NPL's annual reports. The NPL did not publish annual reports from 1971 to 1983 because Sir Keith Joseph regarded them as a waste of taxpayer's money. Nevertheless, the superintendents and scientists of all divisions had to account for their expenditure and the work undertaken annually to the research requirements boards. The only type of report produced by the NPL during this period was its monthly newsletter, which emphasised meetings, conferences, some scientific developments and social events. When the NPL returned to publishing its annual reports in 1984 the format was changed. From 1900 to 1971 the annual reports were straightforward text published either by the Royal Society, the DSIR or the Ministry of Technology. The newly re-established reports in 1984, written for the DTI, were glossy brochures with colour photographs, written in a style that was (and still is) user-friendly.

Despite the transfer from the Ministry of Technology to the Department of Trade and Industry, many of the laboratory's financial problems had not lessened. From 1987 to 1990 the NPL experienced a cutback in finances and this period was regarded by some as an extremely difficult time. An attempt was made to alter the roles of the NPL so that it might become a self-supporting laboratory – an ambition the Treasury hoped would have come to fruition shortly after the NPL was established in 1900. Though there were fewer financial constraints on the purchase of equipment, the Treasury did not give essential funding for staff salaries. Moreover, during this time there was virtually no recruitment at the NPL.

Under the Conservative government of Margaret Thatcher, privatisation polices were being implemented by the Laboratory and around the country. By October 1982 the National Maritime Institute (which was originally NPL's Ship Division, based at the testing tanks in Teddington and Feltham) had been privatised to become British Maritime Technology and six months later, the Computer Aided Design Centre followed suit. The government also called for increased private work and the contracting out of support services.

The support staff at NPL, such as security guards and cleaners became privatised and these services were contracted through various agencies. Rather than making existing support staff redundant, NPL asked the contractor to employ previous cleaners and security guards who had been working at the NPL for many years and who were not under any contract. This form of hiring continued for five years, thus providing some continuity. Further reductions in support staff, such as technicians, occurred when computers became more compact in the 1970s thus eliminating the need for these technicians to undertake laborious readings of instruments. By 1989 various scientists were becoming so concerned about the government's privatisation scheme, that they had to ask the director, Paul Dean, if the government also intended to privatise the NPL. He reassured them that this was most unlikely since NPL's work was, he argued, by its very nature very much a general government responsibility and there were no plans to change their status.

As NPL tried to make itself more financially accountable and continued to receive government funding, more emphasis was put on its work on standards and the overall importance of establishing international standards. It was felt that government officials could understand the concept of standards and calibration, whereas other scientific work which did not impinge on their daily lives, however critical it may have been, might not have been appreciated by such officials. During this time a short film was made by a team of NPL scientists, under the direction of Peter Campion, the deputy director, entitled *Standards in Action*. The film, which was made ostensibly for schools, focused on standards that any government official would

Sir Keith Joseph visiting the Radiation Science Division in 1978, shown with Alan Jennings, Peter Campion and Paul Dean.

Paul Dean.

appreciate – such as those that would have influenced airline safety and radiation therapy. The NPL also began to formulate anecdotal evidence about various standards for ministers. One such example stressed the importance of accurate temperature measurement when loading crude oil on supertankers.

Around this time significant advances had been made by the Japanese in their quality control programmes which put them at the forefront of technological excellence. Their work, in turn, prompted ministers to recognise the benefits of calibration. The government had already established the British Calibration Service (BCS) in 1965 and in 1977 it was transferred to NPL. Although the BCS covered most fields of calibration the NPL divisions continued to offer high accuracy and specialised calibrations, for example, in radiation dosimetry. In 1969 a Calibration Service in Radiation Dosimetry had been set up by the Ministry of Technology; under the DTI this became Measurement of Radiation Science.

Test House

By the spring of 1979, the NPL was proposed as headquarters of the new British Test House Accreditation Scheme. Testing laboratories, or test houses as they were more commonly known, were widely used by British manufacturers, retailers and purchasers (both public and private), to ensure that the goods they had to deal with met appropriate standards of safety, quality, consistency and reliability. Test house customers needed to be assured that the test house they used had adequate staff, equipment and management structure to provide the appropriate level of testing service required. A number of major organisations such as the Ministry of Defence and the Central Electricity Generating Board, already operated schemes of their own for the accreditation of test houses. The DTI thought that the export market in particular would gain from there being a single, national accreditation scheme.

A year later Paul Dean announced that the NPL was to operate a National Testing Laboratory Accreditation Scheme (NATLAS) which was to be launched in the following year. Under NATLAS, accreditation (or, more simply, a formal recognition of competence) was awarded to testing laboratories which met certain criteria relating to professional competence, technical facilities and organisation. While the BCS dealt primarily with the calibration of instruments, NATLAS was to be involved with all aspects of testing and was concerned with establishing that laboratories were competent to undertake specific tests or types of tests. In 1985 it was decided to merge BCS and NATLAS to form the National Measurement Accreditation Service (NAMAS) which provided accreditation for calibration and testing laboratories.

In the autumn of 1984 it was decided that the National Weights and Measures Laboratory (NWML), at Chapter Street in Pimlico, was to move to Teddington. Construction also began for the new building for the Laboratory of the Government Chemist (LGC), then situated

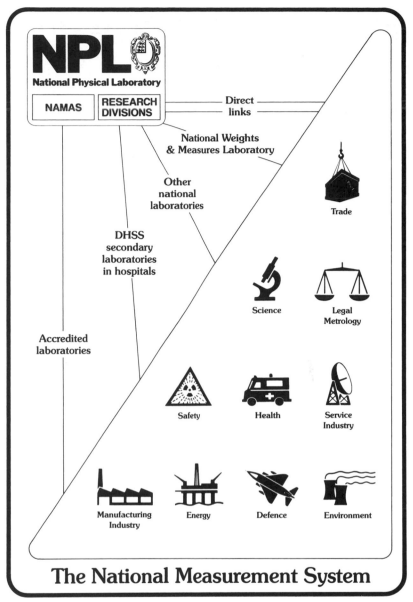

The National Measurement System

Illustration of National Measurement System, 1986.

at Waterloo. The National Weights and Measures Laboratory was responsible for the calibration of the standards used by local trading standards offices to check the accuracy of equipment used in shops, garages and public houses. When LGC moved to Teddington, it became the focus of chemical measurements and standards within the National Measurement System.

Euromet

NPL took a leading role in establishing a new collaborative activity, called EUROMET, which was established in 1988 to further advance international collaboration in the development and dissemination of measurement standards in Europe. This enabled the NPL to maintain links with other national standards laboratories to ensure a consistent measurement system throughout the world. As well as collaborating in Europe, NPL continued to play a major role in world-wide collaborations in metrology, particularly through its active involvement with the International Bureau of Weights and Measures.

In July 1989 the government produced a white paper on the National Measurement System entitled *Measuring up to the Competition*, which provided the national framework of measurement in partnership with business. The white paper was an important policy statement because this confirmed the government's commitment to maintaining a system of national measurement. A year later NAMAS and NATLAS became incorporated into the National Measurement System (NMS) at the Laboratory. As the UK's national standards laboratory, its main function was now seen as providing the metrological infrastructure essential to any industrialised country. Reliable measurements of all physical quantities such as time, length, mass, force, pressure, and capacity were recognised as being of fundamental importance to industry and government alike.

To meet the needs of manufacturers, commerce, health and safety standards, the Executive Committee of the NPL thought that it must establish and maintain a consistent National Measurement System securely based on national measurements and standards, and co-ordinated with those of other countries with whom Britain trades. Reliable standards were recognised as being important to the export and trade sectors. While the Laboratory emphasised its work on standards, the NPL also had to carry out research in certain key scientific and technological areas chosen for their national importance. By the late 1980s, scientific work at the NPL had been reorganised into these six divisions: Mechanical and Optical Metrology, Electrical Science, Quantum Metrology, Radiation Science and Acoustics, Materials Metrology and Information Technology and Computing.

Mechanical and Optical Metrology

The root of all dimensional measurement is the internationally defined unit of length, the metre, which the NPL measured in terms of the

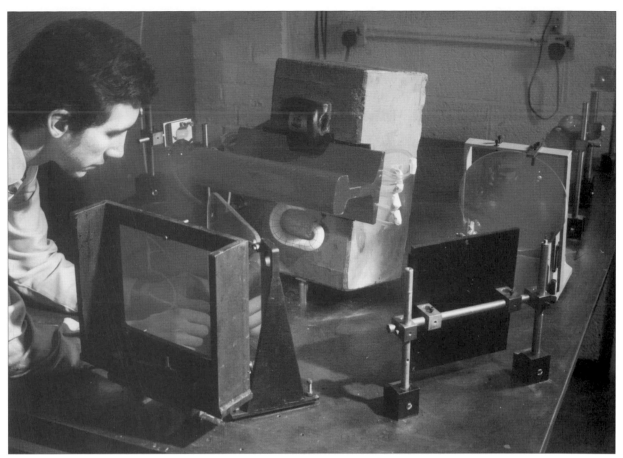

Measuring the deformation of a steel rail clip using holographic interferometry, 1983.

known frequencies of certain ultra-stable optical lasers and the defined velocity of light. The Laboratory also maintains the national standard of mass, the kilogramme, which is compared at intervals with the International Prototype Kilogramme housed at the International Bureau of Weights and Measures in Paris.

With the growing use of computer-linked measuring equipment for quality control in industry (e.g., the co-ordinate measuring machines), the Laboratory was developing facilities for the calibration of three-dimensional artefacts. It also provided standards and calibration services for the following: line widths for semiconductor devices; screw thread forms for the oil industry; particle sizing for paints, ceramics and pharmaceuticals; and angle measurements for gear manufacturing and gyroscope calibration.

The NPL also maintained a wide range of pressure standards extending from ultra-high vacuum to barometric pressures. These standards were employed to provide calibration services to manufacturers and users of pressure gauges and to customer industries (including microelectronics, aircraft instrumentation and power generation). The division also developed and maintained standards for force measurement. The accurate measurement of force is important to many industries ranging from aircraft engine testing to off-shore oil production and other civil engineering applications

Lasers were being used increasingly in optical metrology. By 1984 the Laboratory had developed a range of optical techniques for the measurement of the form and deformation of structures, including photogrammetry, holographic interferometry and *moiré* photography. (Photogrammetry had long been used in mapping aerial photographs.) In 1988 fibre optics had begun to make rapid inroads into telecommunication, instrumentation, local-area networks and avionics. In many applications of fibre optics, the Laboratory recognised that it was crucial to have a good measure of the bandwidth (i.e., information-carrying capacity). In telecommunication, where transmission had become digital, the maximum information transmission rate was usually limited by the spreading in time of each optical pulse as it moved through the fibre.

By the end of 1989, the telecommunication industry was rapidly exploiting fibre-optic technology for the efficient transfer of information at low cost and high speed. In the space of only a few years optical fibre cables, which carried pulses of laser light, had replaced traditional electrical copper cables on city-to-city links within Britain, and were then being installed for some international connections. It was intended that optical fibres would also be introduced progressively into local area networks and possibly directly into the home to increase the range of information and customer services available to the public. Optical fibre systems also found applications in computer data links and local communication networks. It was anticipated that in the future, a wide range of new domestic entertainment and information services would incorporate optical fibre systems.

This new technology required the rapid development of a metrological infrastructure to ensure the highest quality of operation at the lowest cost. To address the need NPL set up an inter-divisional task force to bring together experts in electro-optics, communications technology and optical metrology. The task force liaised with the growing fibre-optics industries to establish priorities and went on to develop the necessary standards and measurement services. Customer demand for the fibre-optic power meter calibration service offered by the NPL greatly exceeded early projections. The problem of increased demand had been met through improvements to basic scale and transfer standards, thus facilitating the introduction of additional calibration services through NAMAS accreditation.

In 1986, the NPL launched a "Nanotechnology Initiative" which related to the manufacture and measurement of components where dimensions of tolerance in the range of 0.1 to 100 nanometres play a critical role. (A nanometre is one millionth of a millimetre.) It promised to make major contributions in areas such as mechanical engineering, electronics, optics and materials technology as the ability developed to control and measure down to atomic dimensions. The Laboratory

NPL mobile laboratory making remote measurements of sulphur dioxide in the smoke plume of an electricity generating station, 1985.

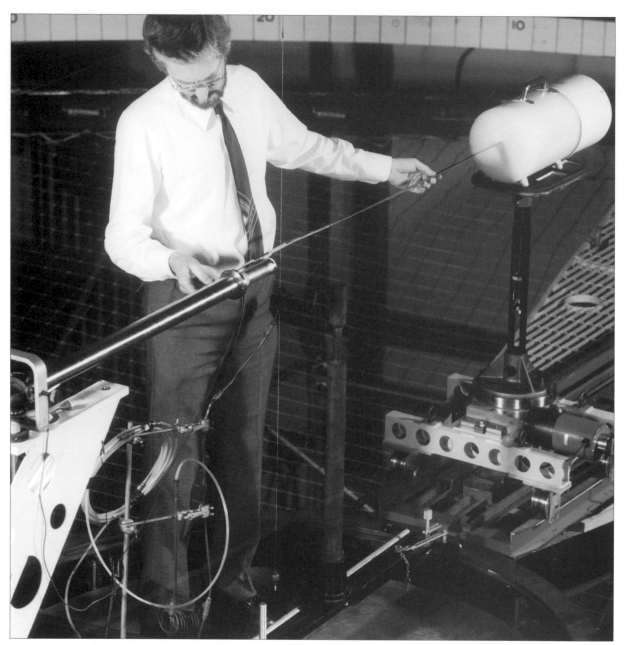

Calibration of a neutron survey meter, 1982.

had first undertaken work in nanotechnology in the 1960s for the benefit of UK industry in the production of X-ray optical components, and the production and measurement of the surface finish of precision bearings, semiconductor substrates and laser gyroscope mirrors.

Quantum metrology

Work on quantum metrology dealt with temperature standards, thermophysical properties, optical radiation measurement, environmental measurement, innovative metrology and fundamental constants.

Environmental measurements began to play a role in the Laboratory by 1984. The concern over the nature and level of pollutant emission into the atmosphere resulted in the introduction of legislation to control industrial, traffic and other emissions. Central to the effective implementation of legislation was a requirement for accurate measurement of pollutant concentration. Powerful new techniques based on lasers had become feasible, and the NPL developed mobile laboratories capable of remote, range-resolved or integrated-path measurement of a wide range of trace gases at distances up to several kilometres.

The accurate measurement of temperature was of increasingly wide concern to industry. Process control, the efficient use of fuel and other resources, quality assurance, condition monitoring, Good Manufacturing Practice (GMP) and the maintenance of healthy, safe and environmentally acceptable conditions all depended on it. On January 1st 1990, the NPL adopted a new International Temperature Scale, ITS-90. The new scale was formulated to incorporate the many advances in fundamental and practical thermometry which had been made in the years since its predecessor, the IPTS-68, was implemented. The numerical values of temperature had been adjusted to bring the scale into closer agreement with thermodynamic temperature.

Radiation science and acoustics

The purpose of the Radiation Science programme was to develop the instrumentation, measurement standards and associated methods needed to enable all kinds of ionising radiation and radioactivity to be characterised quantitatively and unambiguously. In a similar way the acoustics programme was concerned with the measurement and characterisation of acoustics and ultrasonic fields. Much of the requirement for this work arose in connection with health and safety – in therapeutic and diagnostic uses of X-rays, gamma rays, electrons, neutrons, radionuclides and ultrasound, and monitoring the environment and protecting public health.

An accurate measurement of doses was needed for radiation because of the narrow margin between under- and over-treatment. Similarly with ultrasound, now used routinely in hospitals, there was a need to measure the acoustic output of equipment. In radioactivity, the emphasis was on the provision of standards and the determination of a nuclear decay scheme for applications in medicine, nuclear physics and metrology. There was a continual need for new standards as ever more radionuclides, often comparatively short-lived, found applications in medicine and elsewhere.

The Ionising Radiations Regulations 1985, empowered the Health and Safety Executive to approve dosimetry services for both internal and external radiation. While the National Radiological Protection Board (NRPB) was responsible for routine testing of services, it was

Calibration of an ultrasonic hydrophone using a laser interferometer, 1984.

stipulated that the NPL would audit any services operated by NRPB which the board wished to have approved and to carry out tests on other services from time to time, thus providing a direct link with national standards.

Optical radiation measurement provided accurate, traceable measurements of optical radiation, light and colour which were needed for a diverse range of industries and applications. Precise measurements were a key factor in, for example, assessment of developments in lighting technology, quality control in pharmaceutical manufacture and requirements in the newly emerging optoelectronics industry. The NPL began to calibrate hydrophones for medical ultrasound in 1989. One of the most important applications of hydrophones at frequencies in the megahertz range is the measurement of the acoustic output of medical ultrasonic equipment, such as that used for diagnosis and therapy in hospitals.

Among other measures the 1989 white paper, "Food Safety: Protecting the Consumer", included a proposal to allow the irradiation of foodstuffs in Britain which emphasised the importance of a strong regulatory framework for the process. An essential element of this regulation was the insistence that all dose measurement must be traceable to national standards. To meet this demand, the NPL embarked on a programme to provide a reference dosimetry service to the food irradiation industry. The service involved the supply by NPL of dosimeters which, after passage through an industrial irradiator, were returned to the NPL for measurement and certification of the dose received. The service provided a direct link between the normal dosimetry carried out by the operator of an industrial irradiator and the national standards held at NPL. The method of dosimetry that had been chosen was based on the measurement of free-radical concentration in a solid sample. On irradiation, stable free radicals are produced and the concentration of these can be measured by electron spin resonance (ESR) spectrometry.

Fundamental to much of the Laboratory's work in acoustics was the programme on primary standards for airborne sound pressure levels, realised in terms of the sensitivity of standard microphones calibrated by reciprocity. The NPL provided essential technical support to government in the measurement of environmental noises, and the rating of noise in terms of people's responses to it. The development and evaluation of test methods for hearing protectors has also been a responsibility of the Laboratory. As more applications were found for direct voice to computers, industry began to express a need for an independent standardised method of assessing the performance of speech recognisers. The research needed to underpin acoustics, phonetics, computing and the industrial application of speech recognisers in this area provided the means to bring together partners with the relevant expertise and experience.

Electrical science

In order to provide standards in support of the very wide variety of electrical measurement made in virtually every branch of British industry, NPL's work spanned the range from DC to the highest frequencies. The SI unit of time, the second, realised by reference to NPL's caesium standards, is the basis for time and frequency standards. A precise knowledge of time is essential in many fields of technology. Applications ranged from ground- and satellite-based navigational systems to the synchronisation and switching of national and international television broadcasts from different regional centres.

By 1988 accurate microwave standards and millimetre wave standards were much in demand for calibrating the instruments used in checking for possible biological hazards from microwave radiation. Microwave antennas were being used in many areas of radio-frequency technology including radar, weather forecasting and terrestrial and space communications. Calibration of such antennas was required so that the user could predict the overall system performance with some confidence.

Materials applications

Research was aimed at improving the quality, reliability and performance of engineering materials – metals, plastics and ceramics – used by industry. Mainstream activities were directed at measuring properties, protecting surfaces from corrosion, defining the chemistry of interfaces, joining dissimilar components and devising design methods appropriate to new applications of material such as polymers and ceramics. The application of advanced materials was widely recognised to be one of the key enabling technologies which would influence international economic development and industrial competitiveness. Work on materials was carried out within the overall framework of the national measurement infrastructure for materials. The aim was to assist in the improvement of quality, design and reliability of products. The work in this division focused on national needs including statutory and regulatory requirements with a high degree of technology transfer to industry.

177

Determination of the characteristics of a microwave antenna at frequencies above 1GHz in the 10m electromagnetic anechoic chamber, 1987.

The cost of corrosion to the nation was, in 1989, about 4 per cent of the gross national product. To combat this wastage, reliable data was needed on the performance of metallic materials in hostile environments. Plastics and fibre-reinforced plastics are quite different from metals in mechanical behaviour, and new design methods and materials property data were required in applications such as vehicle body panels and bumpers. To study the technical problems in using polymer materials for load-bearing application in vehicles, a consortium-funded project was established. The NPL Consortium on Engineering Design in Plastics was sponsored by BL Technology, Ford Motor Company, ICI Petrochemicals and Plastics Division and the Transport and Road Research Laboratory.

Information Technology and Computing

By the mid-1980s, Information Technology (IT) represented a major industrial growth area with all pervasive applications. In 1986 it was realised that improved means of communication between the computer and the outside world were needed. The programme also addressed the growing range of industrial problems that required technical

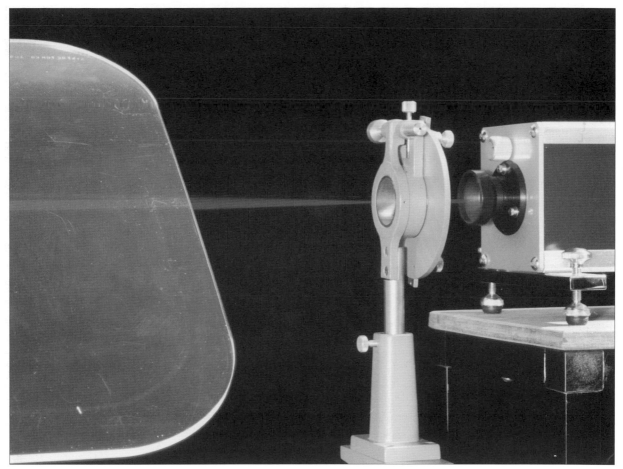

software capabilities in various software libraries. Software testing tools were needed to ensure that users and implementers had compatible systems. Research was directed towards techniques and tools for testing the conformance of systems to standards for open system interconnection . The work was closely allied to that of other groups in Europe and North America. Computer-aided measuring instruments such as co-ordinate measuring machines (CMMs), were widely used throughout manufacturing industry for the inspection of mechanical components. NPL's programme of work included the development of test methods for the validation of computer-aided measuring systems, metrological algorithms and associated software.

Two years later, the Laboratory recognised that information technology was a crucial enabling element in the successful development of British industry and society. Its importance in welding together and sustaining the economic and social well-being of the European Community could hardly be over-emphasised. The NPL programme consequently placed special emphasis on the establishment and effective use of IT standards, and developed the means whereby the performance and quality of IT designs and products could be

Monitoring of residual stresses in aircraft windows by observations of retardation fringes in the scattered light from a polarised laser beam.

179

Microprocessor Aircraft Landing Training Aid (MALTA); a low cost light-aircraft flight trainer developed from original research at the Laboratory.

specified and evaluated objectively. The practical application of computer 'vision' was seen as an important aspect of an extensive British effort in the fields of robotics and automated inspection. So dependent had society become on computers that by the end of the 1980s, the NPL was aware that modern life uses complex computer systems which, if they fail, can threaten life and safety to an increasing degree. Software formed an essential part of such systems and there was a great need to ensure its integrity.

The Next Steps report

When Lord Young became Secretary of State in 1987, he instituted a root and branch review of the DTI's objectives and organisation. He set up a Central Unit under Brian Hilton following the publication of the white paper *DTI – The Department for Enterprise* in January 1988. A month later the seminal report, *Improving Management in Government: The Next Steps*, was published by the Efficiency Unit and announced as Government policy by the Prime Minister, Margaret Thatcher, the following month. The report recommended that suitable parts of the civil service should be transformed into executive agencies, remaining within government but with considerably increased autonomy. Each agency would be headed by a chief executive – appointed from either the public or private sector – who would be given substantial delegated authority to manage the agency in exchange for demanding efficiency and performance targets. In parallel with this development, the Central Unit reviewed the future of all the department's laboratories and identified NPL, LGC and NWML as suitable for agency status; and National Engineering Laboratory (NEL) in East Kilbride, Strathclyde and the Warren Spring Laboratory (WSL) in Stevenage, Hertfordshire as candidates for full privatisation. A more detailed study of the agency proposals was then undertaken by the Chief Engineer and Scientist's Office (led by Colin Hicks) which concluded that the three Teddington laboratories, because of their differing missions, should become separate agencies (rather than a single one). This conclusion was endorsed by Lord Young and formally announced to parliament on June 7th 1988. During 1989, the NPL's major preoccupation was preparing a case for agency status; the subsequent change that ensued in the 1990s will be discussed in the last two chapters.

CHAPTER 18

NPL Management Limited

The 1990s were a period of tremendous change for NPL, especially regarding the increased managerial autonomy of the Laboratory, the more commercial and competitive environment, and the subsequent rearrangement of finances it began to experience. The Laboratory was formally vested as an Executive Agency of the Department of Trade and Industry, by the Secretary of State, Nicholas Ridley, on July 3rd 1990. For the first time in its history, the post of NPL director was advertised in the press and open to applicants from either the private or public sector. In the event Peter Clapham (who was then chief executive of NWML – recently made an Agency) was appointed and he chose the dual title "Chief Executive and Director" – the first to reflect the increasingly commercial environment that agency status was to bring, the second to provide continuity with NPL's distinguished history as an international centre of excellence.

Peter Clapham (left) and Dr Ron Coleman (right) Chief Engineer and Scientist for DTI with Nicholas Ridley declaring NPL an Executive Agency

As an agency, the Laboratory had an increasing degree of autonomy with new management freedom and flexibility. Under this new management, NPL had an agreed operational framework, published performance targets and a more focussed remit. One of its performance

Peter Clapham.

targets was the completion of 90 per cent of customers' calibrations within six weeks: it continuously reached this target so that in 1994, 98 per cent of calibrations were completed on time.

The Laboratory's remit was to serve as Britain's national standards laboratory by maintaining, developing and disseminating standards for all kinds of physical measurement on a consistent and internationally recognised basis. It also continued to serve as Britain's national measurement laboratory, and provide the basis for the National Measurement System. It fulfilled these roles through its standards research, calibration and constancy service, technology transfer, operating NAMAS and supporting the national infrastructure for standard and quality in materials and information technology.

During 1990 NPL had to adapt to the new, competitive environment within which government establishments were expected to function. As an agency, all of the work of NPL was commissioned on a rigorous "customer-contractor" basis, and a greater proportion had to be won through competitive tendering. Thus 1990-91 was the last year in which NPL's work for the DTI was funded directly from money voted by parliament. The following year was the first time the Laboratory operated under the so-called "net running cost control". Under this regime the Laboratory was no longer funded directly from the DTI's vote, but had to recover its full commercial costs through income earned from contracts won from DTI or other customers. In its first year as an agency, NPL won around 75 per cent by value of the work for which it bid, and fully recovered its cost. In this business environment, the Laboratory was successful in developing improved marketing and management skills to complement its scientific strength. The management of the Laboratory was advised by a steering board of senior industrialists and departmental officials under the chairmanship of the DTI's chief engineer and scientist, Dr Ron Coleman.

The majority of NPL's contracts were undertaken for customers within the DTI, all on a strict customer-contractor basis; moreover, the Laboratory had to compete for a growing proportion of its contracts. This change in the way NPL's programmes were funded formed part of the government's policy to create an "internal market" for government research. There were also concerns that the internal market was developing slowly and unevenly prompting a rapid shake out of government research establishments. By 1993, the DTI was actively seeking to widen its range of contractors, and to decrease its dependence on NPL as a prime supplier. NPL's industrial customers also began to see the greater choice opening up in the European market for measurement services.

Nevertheless, the DTI continued to be the primary customer for NPL, accounting for 90 per cent of its work (dealing mainly with measurement-related research and development). Industry, other government departments and the European Commission accounted for the remaining 10 per cent. With the change in management, each scientific division of NPL became a business centre responsible for winning its contracts and delivering its scientific and technical services.

Technology transfer and services

The transfer of technology through links with industrial laboratories and with universities and poly-technics was regarded as a key feature of NPL's work from the early 1990s. There were two primary mechanisms by which this was achieved, including "extra-mural research agreements" under which NPL collaborated with or subcontracted part of its work to outside bodies, and "research investigations" where NPL took on contract research for others. The research investigations typically made use of specialised facilities and provided measurement services which industry could not provide for itself. Other ways to achieve this aim involved: consultancy; clubs in various divisions; contract research and development in collaboration with customers; access to advanced measurement and processing facilities; training courses; and lecturing at metrology courses in various universities.

Electrical science

A wide range of facilities had been established to provide traceable calibrations of optical fibres and components of existing fibre systems. Other developments were planned to cope with new systems that would transmit information at several gigabytes per second. The primary customer for the division's research, development and maintenance of standards was the DTI's National Measurement System Policy Unit (NMSPU). Despite the economic downturn in Britain in 1991-92, the demand for the division's calibration services held up well with more than 900 certificates issued.

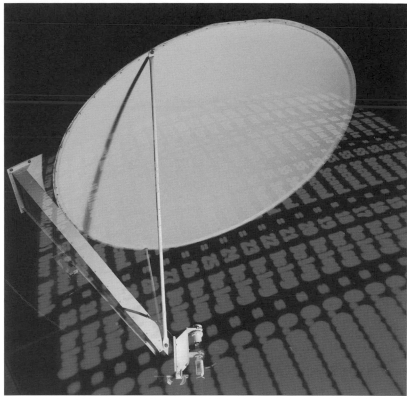

NPL earth station for two-way satellite time transfer.

Measuring the geometry of an optical fibre

NPL's time and frequency services were pivotal to many industries, such as telecommunications, broadcasting and navigation. By 1991 Britain's primary time standards UTC(NPL), were subject to more accurate control as a result of introducing a hydrogen maser to the system. The maser, with its excellent short-term stability, complemented the longer-term stability of the main caesium-beam clocks. By 1994 NPL's task was to support the National Measurement System by providing electromagnetic standards from DC to optical frequencies and also time standards. The majority of demands were in DC and low-frequency AC standards.

The mid-infrared spectroradiometry group had completed a major European contract to develop satisfactory techniques for measuring mid-infrared emissivities of energy-saving coatings on double glazing. This was required to resolve serious disagreements between industrial test houses making such measurements in different EU countries.

The rapid advances that were being made in micro-electronics (particularly the high operating speeds of many personal computers) had increased the urgency for the provision of traceable fast measurements. A calibration service had already been set up for pulse measurement at the 10 picosecond level. (One picosecond (ps) is one million millionth of a second.) These fast electrical pulses had arisen from the development of fast electronic and optoelectronic components and systems. NPL's facility for generating and characterising fast electrical impulses was based on opto-electrical techniques. By 1992 NPL had established a leading place in fibre optics standards in Europe. The optical time domain reflectometer (OTDR) was one of the most versatile and widely used pieces of fibre-optic test equipment. As a field instrument, it was used to locate faults in fibre-optic cable networks.

Microwave integrated circuits were being introduced into a wide range of high-performance radio-frequency and microwave equipment. Electronic components for products such as radar, radio navigation systems, cellular telephones and satellite TV receivers were becoming

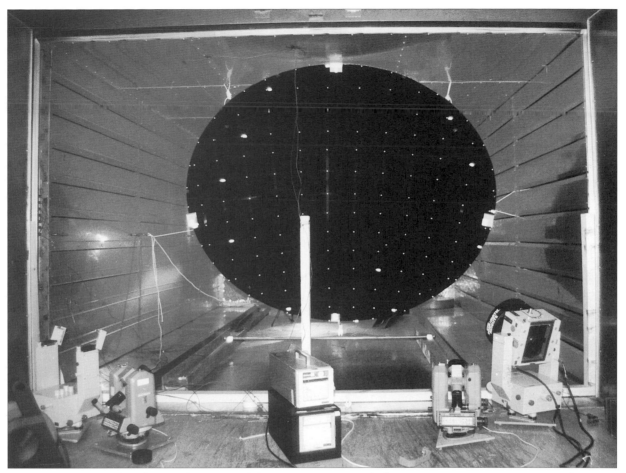

available in microchip form. This opened the way to increased electrical efficiency and reliability, with greatly reduced circuit sizes and lower manufacturing costs. Antenna metrology was largely driven by electromagnetic compatibility and telecommunication needs.

Instantaneous surveying by photogrammetry. By courtesy of Matra Marconi Space UK

Information technology (IT)

By the beginning of the 1990s, all forms of IT systems (in manufacturing, finance, communications, consumer products and transport) were becoming dominated by software rather than hardware. There were still considerable problems in ascertaining whether software was leading to incompatibilities between nominally compatible computer systems. While the National Measurement System underpinned many aspects of standards and quality in the physical world, a similar objective reference structure for software was largely lacking. The term, information engineering, was becoming increasingly used in the field of IT by 1992. This emergent area of engineering dealt with the concepts of specification, design, production and testing, using well-defined techniques with precise assessment of key tolerances and uncertainties. The Division's primary customers were in the IT division of the DTI.

NPL's expertise has helped many uses of safety critical systems. (Copyright Tony Stone.)

By the mid-1990s technology convergence was rapidly becoming the dominant theme driving information systems. Convergence of communication technologies, computer sciences, graphics and presentation design provided innovative products and services for all. The information technology industry, with its rapid rate of advancement, had by 1995 moved into the field of market creation, particularly with original multi-media solutions to both business and leisure needs. The customer demand for the "information superhighway" placed severe demands on the underlying technology, both hardware and software. In a period of a few months, the Internet and the World Wide Web (the practical realisation of the "information superhighway") changed from a mainly academic and research mail and information exchange facility to a vehicle for primary interactive information dissemination. Commercial organisations, governments, technical institutes, schools, colleges and individuals had all become part of the worldwide information culture.

Communication and data security

The demands placed on modern computer systems, in term of interworking, led to the development of a complex set of standards in the

IT field. An open systems inter-connection (OSI) was developed that allowed for an elaborate standards scheme which aimed to provide interoperability and inter-communication for IT products, regardless of manufacturer and communication medium. The OSI standards aimed to achieve the interworking of conforming systems from different manufacturers.

By 1992 further major progress had been made in international standardisation, particularly in the methodology and framework for OSI. Increasing reliance on computing resources means that the consequences of attacks by hackers or malicious software may be severe. Security was thus an important design consideration in the software. Traditionally software relied on the "black-box" approach where test data were fed to the software, and the output compared with expected results. Since it was

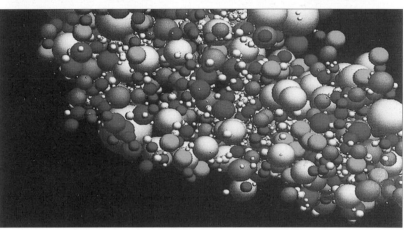

not possible to test exhaustively any but the most trivial programmes in this manner, more rigorous analysis techniques for secure software were required. Changes in the DTI's research priorities resulted in a substantial reduction of funding for IT work at NPL. By 1995 the DTI-funded work was drawing to a close and NPL was seeking to build a robust, technically focused IT development and consultancy business to take its place.

Computer simulation of powder size distribution. Powders are used to make hard metals and are frequently sub-micrometre in size. To make exceptionally strong hard metals even smaller powders are needed.

Division of Materials Metrology

This division occupied a central position in the development and maintenance of Britain's measurement infrastructure for materials. It assisted industry through the improvement of quality, design and reliability of products manufactured using advanced materials or critical process technologies. There was a continuing demand from all sectors of industry for using materials which were both strong and durable. This need was met through the introduction of completely new advanced materials, or by evolutionary developments in well-established materials. For example, the division did valuable work in characterising the properties of "hard metals", some of the strongest materials available to industry like tungsten carbide.

Research was undertaken on the coating of gas turbine blades and power station boilers with corrosion resistant layers for resistance to high temperature aggressive environments.

The importance to manufacturing industries of advanced materials, and the development of methods for their processing, characterisation and specification, was recognised by the DTI, whose Manufacturing Technology Division (MT) was their prime customer. The main programme commissioned by the DTI involved projects for the development and validation of measurement methods and predictive modelling for mechanical and physical properties of advanced materials. Work in this division covered a number of material-specific areas including: polymers and composites; high-temperature materials; ceramics and cements; and thermochemistry.

By the early 1990s there was a strong demand worldwide for harmonised, international standards for advanced composite materials. Environment-assisted fractures represented a major cause of failure and downtime in the chemical, nuclear, aerospace and oil production industries. NPL developed ways to standardise the test methods available for the generation of reliable materials structure and design data, and for models for the prediction of long term behaviour.

Underlying all the research on materials was the firmly acknowledged need for its exploitation. This was achieved through innovative

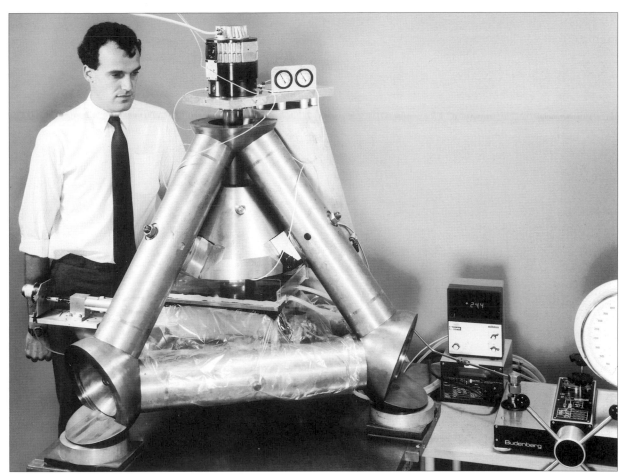

Tetraform 1, a nanoprecision machine tool developed at NPL.

development by industry, through optimisation of processes and through better science-based standards and codes of practice. By 1994 the division was winning over 80 per cent of the projects bid for within three new DTI materials programmes on Measurement Methods for Processability, Composite Component Design and Advanced Materials. All projects had close practical links with British industry through industrial advisory groups, consortia and awareness federations.

Mechanical and optical metrology

Optical standards underpinned engineering metrology as well as the manufacture of optical materials, components and systems. This division provided calibration services for dimensional scales and engineering standards, and for mass, force, pressure, humidity and refractive indices. The division's research programme was mainly driven by requirements for measurement of increasingly small dimensions, for greater measurement accuracy and for automated inspections.

Such measurement accuracy could be attained by micrometrology which provided standards for measurement at the limit of optical resolution (such as, for example, the quality assurance of microelectronic

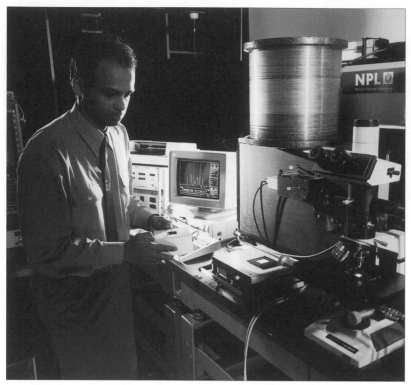

Spectroscopic measurements on active optical fibres.

circuits). Nanometrology was developed to measure capabilities down to atomic dimensions to support a wide range of new technologies such as X-ray optics and ultra-precision machining. Nanotechnology, the technology of manufacturers, has emerged as an important enabling technology, both through its own research programme, and in the Tetraform 1 which was developed as part of NPL's programme on nanotechnology. The tetraform could be used in machine tools and measuring instruments of the highest accuracy. NPL is at the forefront of this development, both through its own research programme in nanometrology, and through its co-ordination of the government's LINK research programme which was able to support collaborative research between industry and the science base. One of the areas of research in 1992 included the application of silicon micro-machining technology to instrumentation for human blood cell analysis.

Computer-aided metrology covered metrological software. New high-performance laser diodes were being used in research on a new generation of ultra-precise frequency standards which found applications in telecommunications and optical information storage. Important machining applications were likely to be found in the manufacture of glass optics and in semiconductors to nanometer tolerances where it is important to limit surface damage introduced by machine vibration. The US Department of Defense delegation identified it as a key new technology in the 1990s.

Division of Quantum Metrology

This division was responsible for developing and providing standards within the National Measurement System in optical radiation measurement, thermal metrology and environmental atmospheric measurements. Accurate, traceable measurements of optical radiation, light, colour and fibre optics were also needed for a diverse range of industries and application. Precise measurements were a key factor in the assessment of developments in lighting technology, quality control in pharmaceutical manufacture and requirements for the emerging optoelectronics industry. The development of all-optical fibre amplifiers for long distance communications led to the need for new

top A 50 kV X-ray facility delivering calibration services to hospitals. **bottom** *Laser pistonphone used in the calibration of microphones at low frequencies.*

measurement techniques for their characterisation.

A Centre for Basic Metrology was established in 1990 to stimulate and co-ordinate the fundamental research required to underpin Britain's National Measurement System. It was also established to provide an in-house focus for NPL work in this area, and to encourage closer links between NPL and higher education institutions. The centre could also carry out research and keep up with the requirements of technological development into the next century. Quantum effects generated in superconductors were investigated, with the aim of linking measurement scales to universal, unchanging physical phenomena defined by fundamental constants.

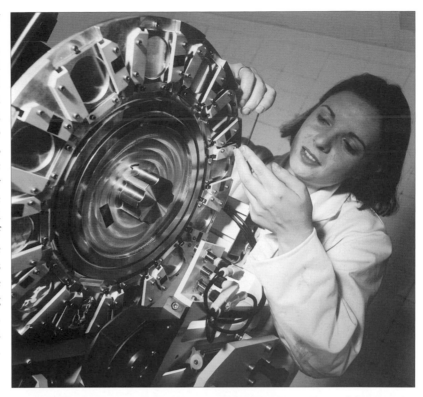

Division of Radiation Science and Acoustics

The division continued to provide internationally accepted measurements in the field of ionising radiation, radioactivity, acoustics and ultrasonics. The need for measurement standards in dosimetry arose from a wide range of users of X-rays, gamma rays, electrons, neutrons and radionuclides. Following continued public concern over the accidental release of radionuclides into the environment, the demand for radionuclide measurement standards at environmental levels has shown sustained growth. In medicine the continuing development of diagnostic and therapeutic applications of radionuclides has assured a steady demand for calibrated standards.

In acoustics, the division maintained Britain's primary standards

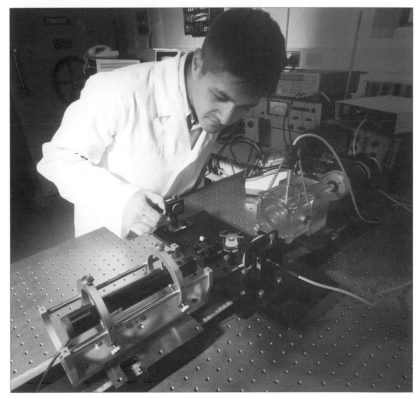

191

NPL's processing expertise and facilities have been used to help customers in the aerospace industry with the production of metal matrix composites.

for the measurement of sound and ultrasound in air and water. Calibration and testing services were provided for manufacturers and users of microphones, sound level meters, audiometric equipment, hydrophones and medical ultrasonic equipment. There were many situations in acoustics which called for the measurement of sound at very low frequencies, and even infrasonic frequencies. Examples included the measurement of noise from quarry blasting, from sonic booms and rocket launches, and wind noises. To enable the calibration of microphones at these low frequencies, NPL developed a laser pistonphone which allows precisely known sound pressure levels to be generated in the frequency range 1Hz to 250Hz.

Aerospace and healthcare

From its position as a broadly-based multidisciplinary laboratory, NPL has developed a dynamic partnership with the aerospace industry, providing research and technical services in many aspects of measurement, materials processing, materials characterisation and information technology. Aerospace is a demanding and quality-conscious sector of industry. It turns to NPL for high level calibration in such fields as metrology, force, optoelectronics, thermal measurement and acoustics.

NPL contributes to health care in a variety of ways. Its audiometric calibration services underpin the diagnosis of hearing disorders and the fitting of hearing aids. It undertakes acoustic output measurement on diagnostic, Doppler and therapeutic ultrasonic equipment. The Laboratory's radiological calibration services facilitate the safe and effective use of ionising radiation and radionuclides in diagnosis and therapy, and also the radiation sterilisation of single-use medical products. NPL also calibrates pressure- and temperature-measuring instruments and ultraviolet (UV) lamps and meters.

The environment

The awareness of the problems arising from air pollution in the early 1990s resulted in international legislation to control air quality and pollutant source emissions. Central to the effective implementation of control legislation is a requirement for accurate measurement of pollutant concentration to understand its effects on the environment. Powerful new techniques based on lasers had been developed which made possible rapid, cost-effective measurement of air pollution. By 1990 environmental legislation was providing increased involvement for NPL with both national and international funding bodies. The impact of environmental legislation resulted in additional work for the EU on the provision of multi-component calibration standards for use with air-monitoring instrumentation throughout Europe.

The concern over the impact of chlorofluorocarbons (CFCs) and other pollutants on the overall chemical equilibrium of the atmosphere, and on the concentration of stratospheric ozone in particular, has increased since the discovery of the Antarctic ozone hole in 1984. Ozone in the stratosphere protects plant and animal life from the harmful effects of ultraviolet radiation emitted by the sun. At high altitudes, the ozone absorbs harmful ultraviolet radiation. Ozone is destroyed catalytically by active chlorine species produced by the interaction of sunlight with CFCs. Moreover, the release of CFCs into the environment has caused complex chemical reactions in the stratosphere and led to the depletion of the ozone layer. In contrast, ozone at the earth's surface is far from beneficial. Ozone damages materials,

A solar tracker in use at the high altitude observatory at Jungfraujoch, Switzerland for the measurement of ozone in the upper atmosphere.

particularly polymers, rubber and coatings and reduces the life of many everyday items with an estimated cost to the British economy in excess of £100 million.

The European Arctic Stratospheric Ozone Experiment, established in 1990, was the latest in a series of international collaborative experiments designed to improve the understanding of the stratosphere, particularly in polar regions. As part of a programme sponsored by the UK Department of the Environment and the European Commission, NPL deployed two ground-based high-resolution instruments at high altitude in central Sweden. They measured the infrared absorption spectra of gases, obtained as the sun's radiation passes through the atmosphere. NPL also made the first ever measurement of chlorine nitrate from the ground using the laser heterodyne technique. As optical radiation became as pervasive as electricity in the technological base of industrialised nations, the resulting diverse range of applications of optical technology created a requirement for measurement standards of improved accuracy.

Environmental issues continue to play a dominant factor in both public awareness and formation of government policy. This has led to a rapid increase in legislation aimed at protecting the environment on both a local and a global scale by exerting tighter control on all pollutant emissions. Growing public concern about the climatic effect of "greenhouse gas emissions" has rekindled interest in energy efficiency, encouraging the development of improved glazing products. By 1994 the need to protect the environment from the consequences of accelerating industrialisation and the impact of consumer economies had received global recognition.

Governments responded by putting into place wide-ranging and stringent environmental legislation, directives and international protocols. These legal instruments set tight limits for exposure which covered air quality, noise, radioactivity and electromagnetic interference. NPL provided measurement standards which enabled industry to demonstrate compliance with these regulations, and in addition carried out work that impacted directly on global issues such as stratospheric ozone depletion and possible global warming through the greenhouse effect. One effect of the pressure of environmental legislation was to force change in manufacturing industry and investment in new processes. As environmental regulations tightened, the control of existing manufacturing processes and existing emissions in the environment was rapidly becoming unviable.

Site development

A decision had been made in 1991 to embark on a substantial programme of rebuilding and refurbishment of NPL's ageing building stock. Many of the laboratories established at the beginning of the century were expensive to maintain and had become quite unsuitable for advanced research work. Plans were being made for a modernised site, fit to take NPL into the twenty-first century. A year later, approval had been given for a major site development programme. By 1994 the emerging design was directed toward a highly efficient, flexible building with particular attention paid to ease of servicing to minimise running costs, while providing for performance to the highest levels as required.

At this time one of the options considered was the replacement or refurbishment of a number of the oldest and least satisfactory laboratory buildings on NPL's site by new, purpose-built laboratories incorporating the flexibility to house a variety of scientific work. In September 1996, Llewelyn-Davis submitted an 81-page master plan, at the request of the DTI. It recommended the refurbishment of some buildings and the replacement of others, but it did not rule out alternative proposals to be considered on their own merits.

Once the DTI costed the refurbishment and replacement of various buildings, it was recognised that this option would be far more expensive than simply demolishing all buildings (except for Bushy House, which is the property of the Crown). It would instead be more cost-efficient to build a new multi-purpose laboratory. Plans were then made to pursue the latter option.

Contractorised management

In May 1993 the president of the Board of Trade, Michael Heseltine, announced a review of the long-term future of the DTI laboratories including NPL. The options he considered included full privatisation, remaining an executive agency or some intermediate arrangement. The *Daily Telegraph* reported on April 5th 1993 that the DTI announced that NPL's £40 million budget was to be cut by about one-third over the next three years. A month later the *Financial Times* reported that Heseltine was considering the privatisation of all the laboratories, including NPL, which were, by then, generating business worth more than £100 million a year. NPL management argued, with the support of its Steering Board and many supporters in industry, that the proposed funding cuts would undermine the operation of the National Measurement System and that privatisation would threaten NPL's independence as a national standards laboratory. These proposed cuts led to further press speculation in 1993 that NPL might have to close down.

Heseltine's plans aroused considerable anxiety among the staff at NPL, especially after he announced the closure of the Warren Spring Laboratory in May 1993 (which was eventually partly transferred to AEA Technology). Later that month Heseltine suffered a minor heart attack when on holiday in Venice. By then NPL had met its primary financial targets, fully recovered its commercial costs and met its vote provisions.

Since 1990 NPL's financial performance had been one mainly of operating surpluses. In 1991-2 the net surpluses were £9.6 million, for 1992-3 it was £3 million, and the two years from 1993 to 1995 were each £3.4 million. When the DTI began to consider repositioning the Laboratory and improving its commercial performance in 1993-4, it paid £1.84 million for investment in business development projects and other restructuring activities. The DTI, with the assistance of KPMG Peat Marwick management consultants, recommended that a private sector team contractor be appointed to manage the work of the Laboratory.

To explore his privatisation options, Heseltine appointed KPMG Peat Marwick in the summer of 1993 to study the commercial potential of the laboratories. In the case of NPL, KPMG recognised the "public good" role of NPL, but also recognised the problem of reduced funding from the DTI, and a high cost base. Its recommendation to Heseltine was that neither full privatisation (as for NEL) nor establishing a company limited by guarantee (as for LGC) were options – the small but real risk of failure was not acceptable. Instead, some form of contractorised management could be explored. In September, Heseltine endorsed this recommendation and asked for further work to be done on contractorisation options. The finely balanced conclusion was that government-owned, contractor-operated (GOCO) was the preferred option. This left the fixed assets (buildings, major equipment) in government ownership, but the staff were to be employed by a private sector contractor who could operate without public sector constraints. On April 14th 1994 Heseltine decided to implement the recommendation by inviting proposals for a management contractor during 1995.

Following a tender exercise, PA Consulting Group was commissioned by the DTI to plan and advise on the project management of the contractorisation process. At a key presentation to the president of the Board of Trade, on June 29th 1994, PA endorsed KPMG's findings that a government-owned, contractor-operated arrangement would be appropriate for NPL. It also argued that any further reduction in the size of NPL would give poorer value in delivering the National Measurement System, and recommended that substantial guaranteed minimum funding from the DTI (over at least five years) would be necessary to secure a successful contractorisation. To the relief of everyone concerned about NPL's future, Heseltine accepted the proposal.

The overall objective in implementing this decision was twofold. Firstly, the DTI wanted to ensure that the Laboratory would still be able to retain and motivate expert staff and to take better advantage of new opportunities. Secondly, NPL was to achieve maximum value for public money (taking into account the restructuring and redundancy costs). The DTI also wished to ensure that certain goals would be met by the private sector contractor, who would be operating the Laboratory as the UK's National Measurement Laboratory in support of the National Measurement System. As an agency of the DTI, the main objectives for NPL were: to remain an important national resource in promoting the competitiveness of British business; to maintain access by government to facilities unique to the Laboratory; to uphold its standing as a world-class centre of excellence in physical metrology; and to exploit its assets, skills and reputation commercially. Throughout this long period of uncertainty over NPL's future, Peter Clapham had been anxious to ensure that the scientific excellence of NPL's work should never be threatened by commercial priorities. He sought and gained the agreement of ministers that, after contractorisation, they would be advised by the Royal Society and the Royal Academy of Engineering on the quality of NPL's scientific output. This initiative, which was announced to parliament on July 14th 1995, re-established a most welcome link between the Royal Society and the Laboratory.

The DTI also wanted to ensure that the final arrangement would be satisfactory to themselves and to the Treasury. After a competitive tendering exercise, PA Consulting Group was appointed in April 1994 to draw up plans to move the Laboratory to contractor management. Notices appeared in The *Official Journal of the European Communities* and the British press requesting expressions of interest. Seven companies and consortia were selected for interview, and five were then invited

John Rae.

to bid. Evaluation of the bids was undertaken by a departmental panel whose aim was to ensure that they met the department's objectives and to establish which would give the best value for money. The evaluation panel recommended that the contract should be awarded to Serco Group plc, a rapidly growing British task-management company which had succeeded in taking complex government institutions into private operation. Today Serco employs some 30,000 staff in 32 countries and is one of the largest employers of British scientists working on government programmes. On July 13th 1995, the DTI signed the contract with NPL Management Limited, a wholly owned subsidiary of Serco Group plc which was set up specifically for this work. The transfer became effective three months later on October 1st. John Rae, who had worked for AEA Technology as head of its energy and environment business and then as the business development director for non-nuclear activities, was appointed by Serco as managing director for NPL Management Limited. With its new status, the Laboratory became known as NPL Management Limited or more simply "NPL".

The contract guaranteed NPL projects from the department to the value of £145.7 million, subject to satisfactory performance, over the five-year life of the contract. Any profits would be shared between NPL and the DTI according to an agreed formula. The DTI retained ownership of the assets which were leased to NPL Management Limited who were responsible for their care and maintenance. From 1990 to 1995, some restructuring was necessary to tailor the size of the organisation. The number of staff employed at NPL had fallen from 821 in 1990 to 535 by September 30th 1995 while still meeting the work demands placed upon them by the government. A significant proportion of these "losses" were due to the transfer of NAMAS to the private sector and further contractorisation of support services. The reduction in staff was achieved through a programme of voluntary early retirement and severance, and natural wastage.

CHAPTER 19

The Future of NPL

As technological change accelerates and commercial pressure on companies to be innovative grows, there has been an expanding awareness of issues relating to quality control. Moreover, a successful industrial economy demands a system by which internationally recognised measurement standards are maintained by a national centre, and disseminated to users by the calibration process. This role has been the basis of NPL's mission from the time the Laboratory was established in 1900. At the end of the twentieth century, NPL has evolved into an internationally respected centre of excellence in measurement research, development and application. The transition to contractor operation in 1995 brought new freedom to develop NPL's work while maintaining the Laboratory, which remains in government ownership, as a national asset. According to the former director, John Rae, and the deputy director, Andrew Wallard, contractorisation has changed the balance of the work at NPL. They also believe that there is more freedom to manage and that they will be able to plan on a longer term basis since the DTI has guaranteed a 25 year lease on the new laboratory.

NPL continues to look for ways to increase the value of its work, both for its principal government customer (the Department of Trade and Industry) and for the increasing number of other clients who contract their services on a commercial basis. DTI funded programmes focus upon meeting needs which no single organisation could fund commercially, and which benefit a wide range of industry sectors. Additionally, there is a growing stream of business awarded to NPL by individual organisations from across the globe, and secured in open competition. This enables NPL to develop as an organisation and to

ensure that the significant costs of operating the Laboratory do not fall entirely upon the taxpayer.

In the words of John Rae, "Sustaining the quality of NPL science is crucial to the viability of national and commercial programmes". This goal is met by the high quality work from scientists and technicians whose ingenuity and ability to innovate is the lifeblood of NPL. Equally important is the availability of facilities that correspond to the quality of staff. The contract to proceed with NPL's new building was signed on July 31st 1998. Construction began at once and should be completed early in the new millennium.

For some years – indeed ever since Lord Young's embargo on industrial work in the mid 1980s – NPL had been progressively increasing its contacts with industry and improving its communications with all stakeholders in the National Measurement System. However, when Rae took up his post as managing director of the newly contractorised NPL, he recognised that these efforts would need to be redoubled given the more commercial environment of NPL's new status. He encouraged NPL scientists to increase their discussions with industry better to understand their problems and find out what long term goals they wanted to achieve. Staff were also encouraged to consider the benefits of their measurement work to all stakeholders. Thus they have to meet the requirements of industry and manufacturing in the UK as well as address measurement issues relating to health and the environment: industry is the *raison d'étre* for the activities of NPL. By the same token, NPL also collaborates with universities which enables the Laboratory to discuss problems of pure physics.

In 1998, NPL won a DTI contract to bring everyone together in Britain who was interested in measurement. The DTI's National Measurement Partnership Programme (NMP) has created a powerful network, linking scientific, industrial and governmental organisations to assure the development and availability of accurate measurement techniques vital to UK competitiveness. Since implementing standard management practices at NPL, which were viewed as quite radical initially, NPL has increased its efficiency and has become more aware of the needs of industry. Many of the changes NPL has undergone parallel those that have occurred throughout Britain during the 1990s; British industry has become more service oriented and more efficient in providing services than it has ever been.

The new NPL building

At the end of 1999 the new NPL building was rapidly taking shape. The laboratory will provide 36,000 square metres of state-of-the-art scientific laboratories, engineering workshops, offices, meeting rooms, an information centre and other supporting facilities, arranged in sixteen interlinking modules. Co-location of all services within one building will increase NPL's efficiency, and maintain its position as one of the world's great national standards laboratories. The scientific areas are flexibly designed to meet NPL's demanding metrology requirements well into the twenty-first century. Special attention is being paid to high environmental stability, low vibration and minimising magnetic and electromagnetic fields. This will thus allow the most advanced standards to be realised, many exploiting effects at the atomic level.

The major relocation project (known as "the decant") has already begun, and most of it will be completed by mid-2001. The decant database currently has entries for 2,800 rooms from which the occupants and contents are to be relocated. Customer care is another crucial activity throughout the decant. It is estimated that 20,000 letters will be sent to measurement services and other customers over the next three years, to keep them in touch with service availability.

As NPL adapts to its new role as a government-owned, contractor-operated organisation, the scientific work at the end of the 1999 was organised into these seven centres of metrology: Basic, Thermal and Length Metrology, Electromagnetic and Time Metrology, Information Systems Engineering, Ionising Radiation Metrology, Materials Measurement and Technology, Mechanical and Acoustical Metrology and Optical and Environmental Metrology.

The scientific centres

The Centre for Basic, Thermal and Length Metrology maintains and develops national measurement standards for thermal and dimensional

The new NPL building, February and September 1999.

201

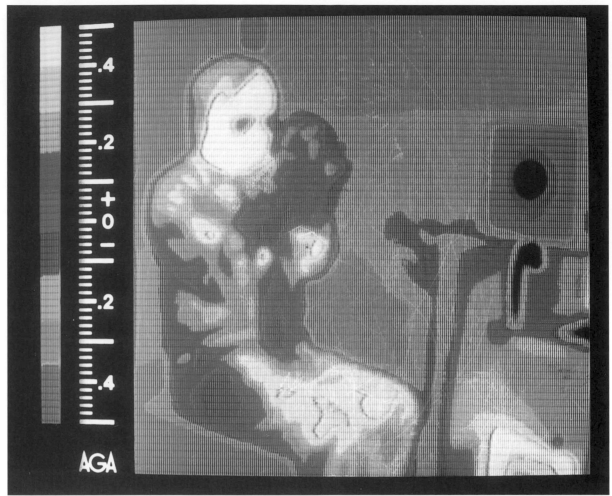

Thermal image of black body during calibration, 1998

top *A neutron personal dosimeter is attached to the face of a phantom in an experiment to evaluate dosimeter response to the backscattered component of radiation.* **bottom** *Underwater acoustic pressure vessel.*

metrology and undertakes leading-edge research into technologies capable of defining the next generation of primary measurement standards. The Basic Metrology group carries out research into the science underpinning future developments in precision metrology, especially atomic and quantum based phenomena and the determination of fundamental constants which underpin several of the definitions within the International System of Units (SI). The Thermal Metrology group maintains and develops national and measurement standards for temperature (the kelvin) from near absolute zero to over 3000°C and maintains and develops standards for the thermophysical properties of a wide range of materials.

The Length Metrology group is responsible for the realisation of the SI unit of length, the metre. It also develops and disseminates measurement standards for engineering dimensional metrology, optical and micro dimensional measurements. The Centre for Ionising Radiation Metrology maintains and develops measurement standards as well as associated methods and instrumentation needed to allow ionising radiation and radioactivity to be characterised quantitatively and unambiguously. The Centre for Materials Measurement and Technology develops methods primarily for materials measurement in support of British industry and trade. The centre is Britain's most advanced laboratory for materials measurement covering a broad spectrum of materials and incorporating a wide range of national and international activities. Extensive facilities are available for characterisation of metals, polymers, sensor and electronic materials, adhesives, ceramics, composites and the assessment of materials behaviour and performance.

The group for Mechanical and Acoustical Metrology devotes world-class expertise and faculties to the provision and dissemination of measurement standards for sound and ultrasound (in air and water), mass, density, force, torque, hardness, extensometry, pressure and vacuum. The Centre for Optical and Environmental Metrology is responsible for the realisation of the SI unit for luminous intensity, the candela, and other primary optical radiation quantities upon which are based all traceable optical radiation measurements within Britain. This centre is also responsible for environmental measurements.

International metrology

In addition to the seven scientific centres, there are other areas of metrology that concern the Laboratory including International Metrology. As globalisation and cross-border businesses increase, various industrial sectors need equivalent and acceptable

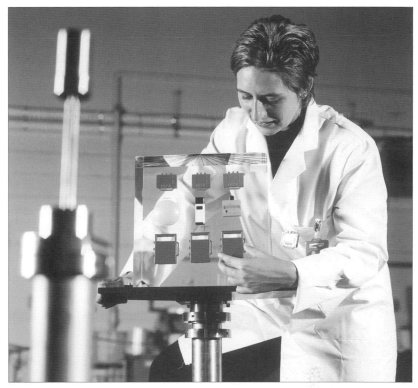

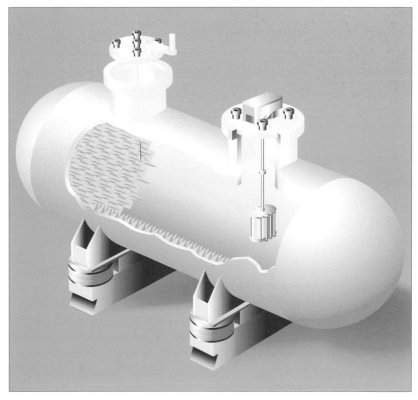

The Pavillon de Breteuil near Paris: the main building of the international bureau of weights and measures. Courtesy of the BIPM.

measurements. Consequently, the many National Metrology Institutes (NMIs) throughout the EU have had to respond and widen their horizon from the domestic market to the international. Much of the driving force for internationalisation has come from an arrangement being co-ordinated by the Bureau International des Poids et Mésures (BIPM) in Paris, to implement the Mutual Recognition Arrangement (MRA) of national measurement standards and of calibration and measurement certificates. This will inevitably bring enormous benefits to British exporters: the NPL signed the Mutual Recognition Arrangement on October 14th 1999.

Inter-governmental bodies such as the World Trade Organisation are recognising the contribution which metrology can make to the reduction of technical barriers to trade and to mutual recognition of tests and calibrations throughout the world. This has driven much of the work of the main international and European bodies over the past year, with NPL playing a central role. Of greatest long-term significance is a plan, co-ordinated by BIPM for the world's major National Metrology Institutes to carry out a series of "key comparisons" over the next five or so years in order to cross-check and validate the ways in which the units and quantities of the International System of Units (SI) are determined.

In this project, which is supported by the EC, NPL are piloting a metrological equivalence database to support the Mutual Recognition Arrangement. The response has been encouraging, and it is hoped that this will remove many of the frustrations experienced by companies when exporting goods from Europe to the USA. By the end of 1998 EUROMET had extended its membership to include the Czech Republic, Hungary, Poland, Slovakia, Slovenia and Turkey as full members, and the Ukraine as a corresponding member. By February 2000, there were 25 members of EUROMET, comprising 24 countries and the Commission of the European Communities.

Meeting the demands of industry

Today's manufacturing and service industries are increasingly science-based and ever more dependent on accurate measurements. In the electrical field alone, the need to make reliable measurements of electromagnetic quantities pervades all aspects of a modern industrial society, from electrical power generation and distribution, through the manufacture of electrical goods and electronic equipment to the use of advanced communication systems. NPL is able to meet the demands of industry by realising the national standards for the base electrical units, and providing an extensive range of calibration and measurement services. NPL provides 26 routine measurement and calibration services for electromagnetic quantities spanning the electromagnetic spectrum from DC to near optical frequencies (including microwave frequencies used in communication and broadcasting, remote sensing and navigation and industrial processing).

Current standards for electro-magnetic radiated emission compliance measurement, on elec-trical or electronic products, require

that such measurements are made either on an open area test site (OATS) or in a semi-anechoic room. Anticipating future needs and undertaking research activities to prepare for them is vital to the health of NPL and the National Measurement System.

The moving-coil apparatus for relating the kilogramme to highly reproducible electrical standards.

Information systems engineering

At the end of the 1990s the development of scientific software has become an important part of the work at NPL. By using their excep-tional mix of mathematical, programming and computer science skills, they are able to solve computation problems for metrologists, physi-cists and engineers which vary from data acquisition through modelling and analysis to visualisation and report generation. The overall theme of NPL's contribution to the field of information systems engineering is "objective measurement, testing and validation". Principally this involves finding applications in providing software and mathematics support to all areas of metrology.

A current topic of mathematical research is data fusion. This seeks to find appropriate mathematical techniques to help make sense of disparate measurement data coming from a large number of different sensors which may be operating under a variety of different condi-tions. For example, in monitoring air quality one might need to monitor temperature, pressure, humidity, concentrations of different gases, the presence of particulates and heavy metals, some of which will vary in systematic ways with time of day, season or weather conditions.

Fibre-optic telephone cable.

Biometrics

Many physiological features such as fingerprints, face and iris patterns are unique to the individual. Measurement and comparison of these features can allow systems to recognise individuals automatically. Such biometric technology is being used in applications such as passport controls, bank machines and building access control. However, the performance of such systems in the laboratory may not reflect what is obtainable in real life. To address this problem, NPL and a group of users and developers of biometric systems, have developed a set of objective performance measures allowing real-world comparisons to be made.

Telecommunication metrology

NPL provides the most extensive range of measurement and calibration services of any national measurement institution to support the telecommunication industry. Terrestrial and satellite communication links and the burgeoning mobile communications sector all depend on radio frequencies (RF) and microwave technologies. The Laboratory also provides measurement and calibration series for power, attenuation, noise and impedance as well as antenna parameters to meet these needs. Focusing on new requirements, they have embarked on a project to develop traceable techniques for the characterisation of the complex waveforms generated in the current Global System for Mobile Communications and future generation systems.

Optical fibres have now replaced copper cables and microwave systems in many point-to-point communication links as they offer higher capacity and lower cost. Current research activities aim to facilitate the exploitation of the immense bandwidth of optical fibres, providing advanced characterisation capabilities and measurement standards for both fibres and a wider range of photonic components. NPL's support of the telecommunications sector is also available through their training and consultancy services. NPL have helped a number of telecommunication operators to establish calibration and quality assurance (QA) facilities.

The Internet and beyond

One of the ways in which NPL envisages change in the speed and efficiency of calibration in the twenty-first century, is through the use of the Internet. It has recently become possible to calibrate remote electrical signals on the internet; this has the advantage of eliminating the need to transport electrical devices or to wait several weeks for the calibration to be completed. The possibilities are still being explored and it remains to be seen what impact the Internet will have on the NPL measurement and calibration system.

Advertising Standards have recently become aware of the capabilities of NPL as they have begun to require that manufacturers test their claims, such as those made by manufacturers of hair shampoo, which promise to make hair shinier than other shampoos. Thus NPL is now trying to measure shininess of hair. The quality of many liquid products, for example, drinks, edible and mineral oils and many pharmaceutical products, are assessed by appearance. Two attributes that are particularly important are the colour and the turbidity (or cloudiness). NPL has recently developed standard measurement services for the calibration of instruments used to measure colour and turbidity in liquids. It has also developed instrumentation to measure gloss, and semi-gloss characteristics of materials and liquids, and new transfer standards for calibration instruments used in industry.

Co-ordinated universal time (UTC)

Britain's national time standard is maintained by NPL. The time standard is based on an ensemble of accurate atomic clocks, active hydrogen masers and time transfer equipment which allows comparison with other time standards around the world. This information is made widely available through the MSF 60 kHz transmissions from Rugby Radio Transmitter Station, and through NPL TRUETIME computer telephone service. NPL is able to maintain Britain's international responsibility for time and frequency standards by contributing to the world time scale, Co-ordinated Universal Time (UTC). By doing this, NPL ensures that the time and frequency measurement system in Britain is fully integrated with that of the rest of the world, an essential requirement for science, trade and communications across international boundaries. The daily time deviation expected from the

Time transfer equipment for the international time system.

most accurate caesium standard today is just 200 picoseconds.

Atomic clocks can keep time to within a few nanoseconds a day, but the year 2000 countdown clock could only be accurate to within a few seconds. The apparent discrepancy arose because the ability to predict the time of the key event – the alignment of the earth and sun corresponding to the start of the year 2000 – was limited by slight irregularities in the earth's rotation. The international time system relies on both accurate clocks and accurate time transfer links to allow those clocks to be compared. NPL has an active research programme to develop an improved realisation of the SI base unit of time, the second, through a "caesium fountain" experiment. The results from the committee that redefined the second in terms of the caesium atom in 1967 have remained robust in the last 32 years even though the ability to measure time has improved considerably since then. Looking ahead to the near future, caesium technology holds great promise for further improvements.

The fundamental limit to the accuracy of caesium frequency standards is set by the time the atoms interact with the microwaves used to trigger the atomic transition. The longer the interaction time, the greater the accuracy with which the second can be measured. Conventional caesium standards shoot a beam of atoms through the microwave cavity, but a new technique uses lasers to cool the atoms, slowing them down from speeds of 200 metres per second to just a few centimetres per second. Inside a caesium fountain standard, clouds of cold atoms are repeatedly launched upwards and then fall back down under gravity, passing through the microwave cavity on the way. The method was pioneered at the Laboratoire Primaire du Temps et des Fréquences in France, and NPL is one of a number of leading laboratories developing the technology. Driven by the demands of industry, NPL are developing greater accuracy and precision (by the microsecond) for time-keeping; this precision is felt to be essential for the Global Positioning System (GPS), computer clocks and radio communication.

The dawn of the year 2000 was a significant event for many people at NPL who invested considerable efforts in protecting their business against any potential Y2K problem. They also have a very special connection with the Millennium through their role in timekeeping. When the Royal Greenwich Observatory was established in 1884, it provided the reference for the first global time, and the term "Greenwich Mean Time" (GMT) was used throughout the world for nearly a century, before Parliament enacted the Co-ordinated Universal Time Bill in 1975. In 1967 the General Conference of Weights and Measures adopted the first atomic second using the regular vibrations of caesium-133 atoms in a clock at sea level as regulator. These atomic clocks formed the basis of International Atomic Time (TAI) and were accurate to less than one second in a million years. In 1975 the International Conference of Weights and Measures, recommended that Co-ordinated Universal Time be derived from the more accurate TAI and become the accepted civil and legal time-scale for

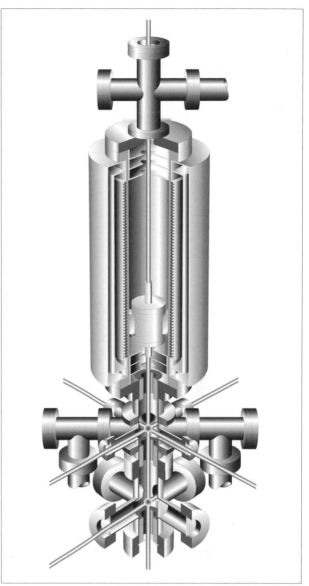

The caesium fountain as a new primary standard.

The NPL caesium fountain.

all nations. UTC could be transmitted from more than 200 atomic clocks around the world with an accuracy of plus or minus two milliseconds. Following these developments for global timekeeping since the 1970s, NPL has been the focus of timekeeping in Britain and will continue to be so for the foreseeable future.

Notes

1. The committee consisted of Alexander Strange, William Thomson (later Lord Kelvin), John Tyndall, Edward Frankland, James Glaisher, George Stokes, H O Fleeming Jenkins, Thomas Henry Huxley, Lord Tennyson, Lyon Playfair and Norman Lockyer.

2. The witnesses included William Thomson, Edward Frankland, Richard Strachey, James Joule, Richard Owen, Alexander Strange, C C Carpenter, George Gore and Warren de la Rue.

3. The MBA grew out of interest in the rising trade in the fresh-fish industry. Three of the MBA founder members, William Turner Thistleton Dyer, T H Huxley and Michael Foster, played key roles in the development of the NPL. Other MBA founding members included W F R Weldon, E Ray Lankester, Adam Sedgwick and J Burden Sanderson.

4. Edward Pyatt, *The National Physical Laboratory: A History* (Adam Hilger Ltd, 1983).

5. The committee comprised Oliver Lodge, professor of physics at UCL; Richard Glazebrook, assistant director of the Cavendish Laboratory at Cambridge University; Lord Kelvin, professor of natural philosophy at Glasgow University, Lord Rayleigh, formerly director of the Cavendish Laboratory; J J Thomson, professor of experimental physics at Cambridge; Arthur Rücker, professor of physics at the Royal College of Science; Robert Bellamy Clifton, professor of experimental philosophy at Oxford University; George F Fitzgerald, professor of natural and experimental philosophy at Trinity College, Dublin; George Carey Foster, professor of physics at University College London, and John Viriamu Jones, professor of physics at University College Wales.

6. The instruments included: thermometers, barometers, hydrometers, magnetic instruments, anemometers, rain gauges, sunshine recorders, theodolites, sextants, compasses and telescopes

7. The committee members included Galton (chairman), Lord Rayleigh, Oliver Lodge (secretary) Lord Kelvin, Henry Roscoe, Arthur Rücker, R B Clifton, George Carey Foster, Arthur Schuster, A J Aryton, T Anderson, T G Thorpe, Francis Galton (cousin to Douglas Galton) and Richard Glazebrook.

8. Russell Moseley, 'Science, Government & Industrial Research: The origins and development of the National Physical Laboratory, 1900-1975', PhD Thesis, University of Sussex, 1976.

9. Eric Hutchinson, 'Scientists and Civil Servants: The struggle over the National Physical Laboratory in 1918', pp373-98, *Minerva*, 1969.
Also see Idem, 'Scientists as an Inferior class: The early years of the DSIR', pp396-411, *Minerva*, 1970.
And Idem, 'Government laboratories and the influence of organised Scientists', pp331-56, *Science Studies*, 1971.

10. Simon Lavington, *Early British Computers. The Story of Vintage Computers and the People who built them,* (Manchester University Press, 1980).

11. See David Yates, *Turing's legacy. A history of computers at the National Physical Laboratory, 1945-1995,* (Science Museum, 1977).

12. Russell Moseley, 'Science, Government & Industrial Research: The origins and development of the National Physical Laboratory, 1900-1975', PhD Thesis, University of Sussex, 1976.

APPENDIX 1: NPL DIRECTORS 1900-2000

1. **Sir Richard Tetley Glazebrook:**
1900-1919
2. **Sir Joseph Ernest Petavel: 1919-1936**
3. **Sir Frank Edward Smith (Acting):**
1936-1937
4. **Sir William Lawrence**
Bragg: 1937-1938
5. **Sir Charles Galton Darwin: 1938-1949**
6. **Sir Edward Victor Appleton: (Acting)**
March to August 1941
7. **Sir Edward Crisp Bullard: 1949-1955**
8. **Dr Reginald Leslie Smith-Rose:**
(Acting) 1955-1956
9. **Sir Gordon Brims Black McIvor**
Sutherland: 1956-1964
10. **Dr John Vernon Dunworth: 1964 -1977**
11. **Dr Paul Dean: 1977-1990**
12. **Dr Peter Clapham: 1990-1995**
13. **Dr John Rae: 1995-2000**
14. **Dr Bob McGuinness: 2000-**

1. Sir Richard Tetley Glazebrook (1854-1935) born Liverpool, son of a local doctor; educated Dulwich and Liverpool Colleges; Trinity College, Cambridge 1872; major scholar 1875; fifth wrangler mathematics tripos 1876; fellow 1877; senior bursar 1895; research in optics under James Clerk Maxwell; appointed demonstrator Cavendish Laboratory by Lord Rayleigh 1879; FRS 1882 at the age of 28; assistant director of the Cavendish 1891; principal, University College, Liverpool 1898-1899. Appointed first director of the NPL January 1st 1900 a post he held until September 1919. Glazebrook carried out important research in aeronautics, notably on conditions of stability, and was subsequently Zaharoff professor of aviation at Imperial College, London 1920-1923. Received the Royal Society Hughes' medal in 1909, the Albert medal of the Royal Society of Arts in 1918, and the gold medal of the Royal Aeronautical Society in 1933. He was knighted in 1917, received the KCB in 1920 and KCVO in 1934 and was the first president of the Institute of Physics.

2. Sir Joseph Ernest Petavel (1873-1936) educated at Lausanne, Geneva; entered University College, London 1893; studied mechanical engineering under T Hudson Bear and electrical engineering under Sir John Ambrose Fleming; received the Solomon's scholarship from the Institution of Electrical Engineers 1896 and a further

scholarship from UCL to undertake experimental work at the Royal Institution's Davy-Faraday Laboratory; established the primary standard of light, and designed the Petavel gauge for measuring pressures set up in exploding gaseous mixtures; John Harling research fellow University of Manchester in Arthur Schuster's laboratory, 1901 and then demonstrator in physics 1906; professor of engineering and director Whitworth Laboratory, Manchester 1908-1919. He became chairman of the Aerodynamics Advisory Committee during the 1914-1918 war, a post he held until 1925. He was a member of the general board of the National Physical Laboratory from 1911 to 1916, and in September 1919 he was appointed its director. During his 17 years as NPL director, Petavel devoted himself to maintaining and increasing the prestige of the Laboratory both nationally and internationally, and increasing its usefulness to various industries in Britain. Elected FRS in 1907 and was awarded the KBE in 1920.

3. Sir Frank Edward Smith (1876-1970) an industrial scientist, educated at Smethwick Central School and the Royal College of Science; first class honours in physics 1899; assistant to Glazebrook at the NPL, Kew Observatory in 1900; research on accurate electrical standards and methods of measurement; constructed first 'Lorenz' machine; established standard units; FRS in 1918; director, Scientific Research and Experimental Department, Admiralty 1920; supervised construction of Admiralty Research Laboratory, Teddington. Acting director of the NPL from 1936-1937 and received an OBE, 1918; CBE, 1922; CB, 1926; KCB, 1931; GBE, 1939 and GCB, 1942.

4. Sir William Lawrence Bragg (1890-1971) elder son of Sir William Henry Bragg; educated at Queen's Preparatory School and St. Peter's College, Adelaide, Australia; first-class honours mathematics, 1908; went to Trinity College, Cambridge 1909, first class mathematical tripos (part i) and natural science tripos (physics) (part ii); fellow of Trinity College and in 1914, a lecturer of the University; worked on X-ray analysis of crystal structures and determined the atomic arrangements of sodium and potassium chlorine; with his

father, William, he determined the structure of the diamond and father and son were jointly awarded the Nobel Prize for this work; succeeded Lord Rutherford as Langworthy professor of physics at Manchester 1919; elected FRS 1921. He was appointed director of the NPL in 1937 and then succeeded Rutherford as Cavendish professor of physics at Cambridge in 1938. From 1954 to 1966, he was director of the Davy-Faraday Laboratory at the Royal Institution. Bragg was awarded an MC and an OBE in 1918 and the Copley medal in 1966 from the Royal Society. He received honorary degrees from 11 universities, was knighted in 1941 and received the CH in 1967.

5. Sir Charles Galton Darwin (1887-1962) mathematical physicist and the son of George Darwin, FRS and grandson of the evolutionary biologist, Charles Robert Darwin, author of the Origin of Species (1859). Darwin was educated at Marlborough College and Trinity College, Cambridge; fourth wrangler, mathematical tripos 1910; joined Ernest Rutherford and Niels Bohr as the Arthur Schuster lecturer in mathematical physics at Manchester 1910-12; worked with H G J Mosley on the diffraction of X-rays for two years; served with the Royal Engineers and the Royal Flying Corps; fellow and lecturer at Christs College, Cambridge 1919-1922, and became Master of the college in 1936. From 1924 he was Tait professor of natural philosophy at Edinburgh University. Darwin was director of the NPL from 1938-1949 and played an important role in reorganising the NPL after the 1939-1945 war. He was made an FRS in 1922, and was the president of various societies including the Physical Society (1941-44) and the Eugenics Society (1953-59). He received the KBE 1942 and also received honorary degrees from Manchester, St Andrews College and Trinity College, Dublin.

6. Sir Edward Victor Appleton (1892-1965) educated at Hanson School, Bradford and St. John's College, Cambridge; first class honours in the natural science tripos 1914; fellow of St John's College 1919; assistant demonstrator in physics at the Cavendish Laboratory 1920; undertook research on radio waves and the ionosphere; Wheatstone professor of physics at King's College,

London 1924-1936; Jacksonian professor of natural philosophy at Cambridge 1936-1939; secretary of the Department of Scientific and Industrial Research 1939-1949; closely concerned with the development of radar and secret work on the atomic bomb. When Charles Darwin was seconded to the position of director of the Central Scientific Office, British Supply Council, in Washington DC, during the 1939-1945 war, Appleton became acting director of the NPL from March to August 1941. He was knighted in 1941, was awarded the Nobel Prize in 1947.

7. Sir Edward Crisp Bullard (1907-1980) educated at Repton School and Clare College, Cambridge; first class honours in both parts of the natural science tripos specialising in physics1929; research student at the Cavendish Laboratory 1929-1931; demonstrator of geodesy and geophysics 1931; PhD 1932; Smithson research fellow of the Royal Society 1936-1943; joined HMS Vernon, a naval mine station, 1939; undertook investigations into magnetic mines and the demagnetising of ships; fellow of Clare College, Cambridge 1943; reader in experimental geophysics Cambridge 1945-1947; professor of physics Toronto University 1947-1949; Sc.D. 1948.In 1950 he became director of the NPL until 1956. He was then senior research fellow at Gonville and Caius College, Cambridge and subsequently assistant director of research 1956-60. He was afterwards reader and then first professor of geophysics at Cambridge. He was made FRS 1941, knighted 1953, received the Day medal of Geological Society of America 1959 and the Royal medal of the Royal Society in 1975.

8. Reginald Leslie Smith-Rose (1894-1980) educated at Latymer Upper School, Hammersmith, West London and Imperial College, London; first class honours physics 1914; assistant engineer at Siemens Brothers of Woolwich 1915-1919; joined the NPL 1919; PhD 1923; D.Sc 1926. Twenty years after first joining the NPL, he became superintendent of the Radio Department for eight years until becoming director of the Radio Research Station at Ditton Park 1948-1960. During his time at Ditton he became a world leader on radio direction-finding. He was acting director of the NPL from 1955-1956 and received the US Medal of Freedom with silver palm in 1947 and CBE in 1952.

9. Sir Gordon Brims Black McIvor Sutherland (1907-1980), educated at Morgan Academy, Dundee and at St Andrews University; first class honours MA mathematics 1928; BSc physics 1929; scholarship to Trinity College, Cambridge and worked with Ralph H Fowler; spent two years at the

University of Michigan working on the vibrations and rotations of molecules; returned to Cambridge and collaborated with W G Penney on infra-red and Raman spectroscopy; awarded the Stokes studentship of Pembroke College, Cambridge 1934; fellow 1935; during the 1939-1945 war worked on bomb disposal, and with a research group in Cambridge to identify main sources of fuel mixtures used by enemy aircraft, reader in spectroscopy Cambridge 1947; professor of physics University of Michigan, 1949. From 1956-1964 he was director of the NPL and afterwards master of Emmanuel College, Cambridge,1964-1977. He was elected as an FRS 1949, knighted 1960 and was the vice-president of the Royal Society from 1961-1963.

10. John Vernon Dunworth (born February 24th 1917) nuclear physicist; educated at Manchester Grammar School and Clare College, Cambridge; Twisden studentship and fellowship Trinity College, Cambridge 1941; during the 1939-1945 war assisted the Ministry of Supply in radar development; National Research Council, Canada, working on atomic energy 1944-1945; demonstrator in physics at Cambridge 1945-1947; joined the Atomic Energy Research Association at Harwell. He was director of the NPL from 1964-1976 and was awarded the CB and CBE.

11. Paul Dean (born January 23rd 1933) educated at Hackney Downs Grammar School; and Queen Mary College, University of London; BSc first class honours and PhD in physics; joined the NPL in 1957 in the Mathematics Division; head of the Central Computing Unit in 1967; superintendent of the Division of Quantum Metrology, 1969; deputy director 1974-1976; director 1977-1990. As director of the NPL he was responsible for initiating testing laboratory accreditation in the UK, which led to the development of NAMAS in 1985. He was a member of the International Committee of Weights and Measures from 1985 to 1990 and a founder member and president of the British Measurement and Testing Association from 1990 to 1995. With the current deputy director, Andrew Wallard, he helped to establish EUROMET, which was set up to further advance international collaboration in the development and dissemination of measurement standards in Europe.

12. Peter Clapham (born November 3rd 1940) educated at Ashville College, Harrogate. BSc in physics at University College London 1960, PhD in optics 1969, Imperial College. After receiving his PhD, he pursued research in laser applications and precision engineering at the NPL. He was then promoted to Marketing Director of NPL and during this time he doubled the Laboratory's industrial

income. Following this work, he moved to Whitehall in Technology Policy, a division of the Department of Trade and Industry. He returned to NPL as division head to improve industrial relevance of work, customer responsiveness and international collaboration. He became director of the National Weights and Measures Laboratory in 1985 and director and chief executive of the NPL in 1990. During Clapham's five years as director, he managed the Laboratory through a fundamental process of change in preparing it for private sector operation. This involved introducing substantial efficiency improvements, quality management procedures and commercial disciplines, while maintaining scientific excellence, staff motivation and NPL's reputation for integrity. He is now a self-employed consultant in the fields of metrology, standard, testing and conformity assessment.

13. John Rae (born September 29th 1942) trained as a physicist and was educated at Rutherglen Academy and University of Glasgow; BSc first class honours in mathematical & natural philosophy 1964; PhD in theoretical physics 1967. From 1964 to 1974 he was a lecturer and researcher in physics at Glasgow, the University of Texas at Austin, University Libre and Queen Mary College, University of London. He then joined the Atomic Energy Research Establishment at Harwell where he was industrial fellow from 1974-76; leader of the theory of fluids group in the Theoretical Physical Division and then acting division head 1985. From 1986-1989 he was chief scientist for the UK Department of Energy. In 1990 he was chief executive of AEA Environment & Energy; from 1993 to 1995 he was business development director for non-nuclear activities at AEA Technology. Managing director of NPL Management Ltd from 1995 to 2000, he is now chief executive of AWE Management Limited.

14. Bob McGuiness (born December 31st 1951) educated at St. Mirin's Academy, Paisley and University of Glasgow; BSc honours chemistry 1973 and PhD polymer chemistry 1976. He worked for the ICI PLC group for 24 years, beginning in 1976, in various roles ranging from research scientist, business manager to chief executive. He had postings in Slough, Berkshire; Hilden, Germany and Cleveland, Ohio USA. During his time at ICI, McGuiness motivated and led staff and management teams in the UK, Germany and the USA to improve business performance. He also built businesses and managed successful relations across diverse sectors including auto manufactures, insurance companies, rail, aircraft, steel and aluminium industries. He was appointed managing director of NPL in 2000.

APPENDIX 2: THE DIVISIONAL ORGANISATION OF NPL 1900-2000

1900-1908
Three departments with divisions:
Physics Department – Electricity & Magnetism, Metrology, Optics & Photometry, Thermometry, Metallography and Chemical Tests.
Engineering Department
Observatory Department – Magnetic Observations, Meteorological and Seismological work.

1908-1912
Physics – Electricity, Electrotechnics including photometry, Thermometry, Metrology and Optics.
Engineering
Observatory – at Kew in Richmond and the Eskdalemuir Observatory.
Metallurgy and Metallurgical Chemistry
William Froude National Tank

1912-1918
Physics – Electricity, Electrotechnics, Heat, Metrology, Optics, Radium and Tide Predictions.
Engineering – Aeronautics, Road Research Laboratory, Test work.
Metallurgy and Metallurgical Chemistry
William Froude National Tank

1918-1932
Seven departments with divisions and sub-divisions:
Physics – Heat: Thermometry, Pyrometry, Thermal Properties.Optics: Optical Theory, Instruments, Calculations. Sound. Molecular Physics. Radium and X-rays – renamed Radiology in 1931.
Electricity – Electrical Measurements; Electrotechnics including Direct Current, Alternating Current and Photometry; Wireless.
Metrology – Standards of Length, Gauges, Instruments, Glassware.
Engineering – Strength of Materials, Fluid Resistance & Hydraulics, Heat,

Engines & Mechanisms, Road Board.
Metallurgy – Ferrous, Non-ferrous, Glass & Refractories, Chemistry.
Tank – Ship Trials, Aero-experiments.
Aerodynamics

1933-1939
Eight departments with divisions:
Physics – Heat, Optics, Acoustics, and Molecular Physics.
Metrology – Measurement of Length, Area,Volume, Mass and Time.
Electricity – Photometry.
Engineering
Froude Tank Laboratory
Aerodynamics
Metallurgy
Radio

1940-1945
Ten departments with divisions:
Physics – Heat, Acoustics, and Molecular Physics.
Metrology – Measurement of Length, Area,Volume.
Mass and Time
Electricity
Engineering
Froude Tank Laboratory
Aerodynamics
Metallurgy
Radio
Light – created in 1940 by combining the Optics Division from Physics and the Photometry Division from Electricity.
Mathematics – created in 1945.

1946-1951
Post-war developments. Areas now called divisions with sub-divisions:
Physics – Heat, Acoustics, and Molecular Physics.
Metrology – Measurement of Length, Area, Volume, Mass and Time.
Electricity – Dielectrics, High Voltage.
Engineering
Froude Tank Laboratory
Aerodynamics

Metallurgy
Radio
Light
Electronics – created in 1946, formed part of Radio Division in 1947 and became independent section in 1948.
Mathematics – ACE, General Computing, Differential Analysers. 1945.
Test House – created in 1951.

1952-1958
Physics – Heat, Temperature Measurement, Acoustics & Sound Measurement, Ultrasonics, High Pressure, Radiology, Engineering.
Metrology – Physical Measurements, Engineering Measurements, Control Mechanisms.
Electricity – Dielectrics, High Voltage.
Light – General Optics, Colorimetry, Photometry, Radiometry, Photographic Research, Polarimetry, Research on Vision.
Engineering – moved to National Engineering Laboratory, East Kilbride in 1952.
Ship – Tank project, Hull & Propeller Designs.
Aerodynamics – Aerofoil, High-speed Flow Research, Aircraft control, Fluid Motion Research.
Metallurgy – Refractories, Elastic and Plastic Deformation of Metals, Creep of Metals, Chemistry and Titanium, Magnesium, Chromium & Uranium.
Radio – moved to Radio Research Station in 1952.
Electronics – Computer and Applications.
Mathematics – ACE, General Computing, Differential Analysers.
Test House

1958-1962
The 1960s heralded the emergence of 'Big Science'. Consequently, the NPL reorganised its scientific divisions three times in the 1960s:

Basic Physics – Heat and Thermometry, High Pressure, Ultrasonics, Strength of Materials.
Applied Physics – General Physics, Radiology, Acoustics, Electrotechnics, High Voltage and The Test House.
Standards – Electrical and Frequency Measurements, Temperature Measurements, Pneumatic Gauging, Load Measurements, Hardness Measurement.
Ship – Hydrodynamics at Feltham, Ship Models, Motion of Ships, Hull and Propeller Design.
Aerodynamics – Aerofoil, High-speed flow research, Aircraft control, Fluid Motion Research.
Light – Colour Vision, Photometric Standards, Radiometric Photometry, Radiometric Tests, Colour Temperature Scale, Applied Photometry and Colorimetry, Diffraction Gratings.
Metallurgy – Fatigue, Niobium, X-Ray, Metal Physics, Chemistry, Thermodynamics of Alloys.
Mathematics – Numerical Methods Group, Applied Mathematics Group, General Computing Group.
Control Mechanisms and Electronics – Computing techniques, ACE, Clerical Mechanization, Non-linear Systems.

1962-1965

New subdivisions were created for the NPL's major divisions:
Applied Physics – Radiology, Acoustics, Electrotechnics, the Test House and High Voltage.
Light – Optics, Radiation and Standards, Applied Photometry and Colorimetry.
Mathematics – Numerical Methods Group, Applied Mathematics Group, General Computing Group.
Metallurgy – Metal Physics, X-ray analysis, Mechanical Properties, Iron Alloys, Non-ferrous Metals and Alloys plus Chemistry.
Standards – Physical, Electrical and Mechanical.

1965-1987

Following the amalgamation of the NPL and the NCL in 1965, the combined laboratories were organised into three groups:
Measurement Group – Metrology Centre, Quantum Metrology, Electrical Science, Optical Metrology and Radiation Science.
Materials Group – Chemical Science, Inorganic and Metallic Structure, Materials Application and Molecular Sciences.
Engineering Sciences Group – Aerodynamics, Acoustics, Numerical and Applied Mathematics, Computer Science and Central Computing Unit, Ship Division and Hovercraft Unit. (The Ship Tank at Feltham was privatised in October 1982 and became the National Maritime Institute.)

1987-1998

By 1987, scientific work at the NPL was organised into six divisions:
Mechanical and Optical Metrology – engineering metrology, covering dimensional, mechanical and optical measurements.
Electrical Science – electrical metrology from DC to the highest frequencies.
Quantum Metrology – thermal metrology, optical radiation, standards, atmospheric measurements, innovative metrology and fundamental constants.
Radiation Science and Acoustics – metrology for ionising radiation, acoustics and medical and industrial ultrasound.
Materials Metrology – engineering materials, surface properties and corrosion.
Information Technology and Computing – standards for IT, human-machine interaction and numerical software.

1999 - Present

In its new role as a government-owned contractor-operated organisation, seven centres of metrology were organised at the end of 1999:
Basic Thermal and Length Metrology – maintains and develops national measurement standards for thermophysical properties and dimensional metrology; the Length Metrology is responsible for engineering dimensional metrology, optical and micro-dimensional measurements.
Electromagnetic and Time Metrology – involves precision metrology, especially atomic and quantum based phenomena and the determination of fundamental constants which underpin the SI (the international system of units).
Information Systems Engineering – development of scientific software using mathematical, programming and computer science skills.
Ionising Radiation Metrology – maintains and develops methods and instrumentation needed to allow ionising radiation and radioactivity to be characterised quantitatively and unambiguously.
Materials Measurement and Technology – covers a broad spectrum of materials and incorporates a wide range of national and international activities. Extensive facilities are available for characterisation of metals, polymers, sensor and electronic materials, adhesives, ceramics, composites and the assessment of materials behaviour and performance.
Mechanical and Acoustical Metrology – provides and disseminates measurement standards for sound and ultrasound (in air and water), mass, density, force, torque, hardness, extensometry, pressure and vacuum.
Optical and Environmental Metrology – determines the SI unit for luminous intensity, the candela, and other primary optical radiation quantities upon which are based all traceable optical radiation measurements within Britain.

BIBLIOGRAPHY

Annual Reports:

Annual Reports of the NPL, Executive Committee Minutes, 1899-1945.

Annual Reports of the National Physical Laboratory, Department of Scientific and Industrial Research, 1917-1964.

Public Record Office, Department of Scientific and Industrial Research Files in DSIR 10-17, and Treasury Files T161 and T165.

Annual Reports of the National Physical Laboratory, Ministry of Technology, 1965-1970.

NPL Annual Report, Department of Trade and Industry 1984-1990.

NPL Annual Report and Accounts, Department of Trade and Industry, 1991-1995.

NPL Annual Review, Department of Trade and Industry, 1996-1999.

The Royal Society, National Physical Laboratory files.

Parliamentary Reports:

Eighth Report of the Royal Commission on Scientific Instruction and the Advancement of science. The Devonshire Commission, Parliamentary Papers, C. 1298, xxviii (1875).

Government Scientific Organisation in the Civilian Field, Advisory Council on Scientific Policy (HMSO, July 1951).

Report for a Committee of Enquiry, DSIR (1956).

Industrial Research and Development in Government Laboratories: A new Organisation for the Seventies, The Ministry of Technology (HMSO, 1970).

A framework for Government Research and Development, The Rothschild Report, Cmnd. 5046, (1972).

Technical Services for Industry, Ministry of Technology, (1966-1975).

Articles and Books:

Bernal, John Desmond, *The Social Function of Science* (Routlege, 1939).

Bourn, John, 'Report of the Comptroller and Auditor General: The contractorisation of the National Physical Laboratory', *NPL Reports and Accounts* (DTI, 1995).

Brewster, David, 'The British Association for the Advancement of Science', *The North British Review*, 14, pp235-87 (1850).

Galton, Douglas, 'On the Reichsanstalt, Charlottenburg, Berlin', *Report of the Sixty-Fifth Meeting of the British Association for the Advancement of Science,* pp606-08 (John Murray, 1896).

Glazebrook, Richard Tetley, 'The aims of the National Physical Laboratory of Great Britain', *Annual report of the Board of Regents of the Smithsonian Institution, 1901,* pp341-57 (Washington D C: Government Printing Office, 1902).

Heath, Frank, 'The government and the organisation of scientific research', *Journal of the Royal Society of Arts*, 67, pp206-15 (1918-1919).

Lockyer, Norman, *Education and National Progress* (Macmillan, 1906).

Rayleigh, Lord, *Lord Balfour in his relation to science* (Cambridge University Press, 1930).

Rosenhain, Walter, 'The National Physical Laboratory: Its work and aims', *Journal of the West of Scotland Iron and Steel Institute,* pp1-50 (1915-16).

Schuster, Arthur, *The progress of physics, 1875-1918* (Cambridge University Press, 1911).

Strange, Alexander, 'On national institutions for practical scientific research', *Quarterly Journal of Science,* pp38-50 (1869).

Thomas, J J, *Recollections and Reflections* (Bell, 1936).

Watson-Watt, Robert, 'The evolution of radiolocation', *Journal of the Institution of Electrical Engineers,* Part 1 93, pp374-82 (1946).

'Early Days at the National Physical Laboratory', a lecture delivered at the Laboratory on March 23rd 1933 (NPL, 1933, reprinted 1970).

'A modern scientific industry', *Nature*, 63, pp173-74 (1900).

'The National Industrial Research Laboratory', *Engineering*, 105, pp252-56 (January-June, 1918).

'The Physikalisch-Technische Reichsanstalt: Fifty Years of Progress', *Nature*, 142, pp352-54 (1938).

'Presidential Address to the British Association, 1895', *Report of the Sixty-Fifth Meeting of the British Association for the Advancement of Science, pp3-25* (John Murray, 1896).

'Science and Industry with special reference to the work of the NPL', an address to the Birmingham and Midlands Institute, December 4th 1916.

Secondary Sources:

Barrell, H, 'A short history of measurement standards at the National Physical Laboratory', *Contemporary Physics,* 9, pp171-80 (1969).

Cahan, David, *An Institute for an Empire* (Cambridge University Press, 1989).

Cambell-Kelly, Martin, 'Programming the Pilot ACE: Early programming activity at the National Physical Laboratory', *Annals of the History of Computing,* 3, pp133-162 (1981).

Davies, John Langdon, NPL, *Jubilee book of the National Physical Laboratory* (HMSO, 1950).

Edgerton, David, *Science, technology and the British industrial 'decline', 1870-1970* (Cambridge University Press, 1996).

Foreman, Susan, *Shoes and Ships and Sealing Wax: An illustrated history of the Board of Trade 1786-1986* (HMSO, 1986).

Gowing, Margaret, *Britain and Atomic Energy 1939-1945* (Macmillan, 1964).

Hailsham, Lord, 'Science and government in a free society', *Nature,* 192, pp393-98 (1961).

Hobsbawn, E J, *Industry and Empire* (Penguin, 1969).

Hutchinson, Eric, 'Scientists and Civil Servants: The struggle over the National Physical Laboratory in 1918', *Minerva,* 7, pp373-98 (1969).

Lavington, Simon, *Early British Computers: The Story of Vintage Computers and the People who built them* (Manchester University Press, 1980).

MacLeod, Roy, 'Public Science and Public Policy in Victorian England', *Minerva,* 4, pp197-230 (1971).

MacLeod, Roy and Andrews, E K, 'The origins of the DSIR: Reflections on ideas and men, 19115-16', *Public Administration*, pp23-48, Spring 1970.

Magnello, M Eileen, 'The non-correlation of biometrics and eugenics: Rival forms of laboratory work in Karl Pearson's career at University College London', *History of Science,* 37, pp123-150, 79-106 (1999).

Morrell, J B, 'The patronage of mid-Victorian science in the University of Edinburgh', *Science Studies,* 3, pp353-88 (1973).

Moseley, Russell, 'Science, Government & Industrial Research: The origins and development of the National Physical Laboratory, 1900-1975', PhD Thesis, University of Sussex, 1976.

Pankhurst, R C, 'Aerodynamics at NPL, 1917-1970', *Nature,* 238, pp375-80 (1972).

Pyatt, Edward, *The National Physical Laboratory. A History* (Adam Hilger Ltd, 1983).

Smith, E E, *Radiation Science at the National Physical Laboratory, 1912-1955* (HMSO, 1975).

Smith-Rose, R L, 'Early days in radio research', *Electronics and Power,* 13, pp253-58 (1967).

Snow, C P, *Science and Government* (Oxford University Press, 1961).

Varcoe, Ian, 'Scientists, government and organised research: The early history of the DSIR, 1914-16', *Minerva,* 8, pp192-217 (1970) .

Weinberg, Alvin M, *Reflections on Big Science* (Pergamon, 1967).

Wersky, Gary, 'Scientists and outsider politics', *Science Studies,* 1, pp67-83 (1971).

Wilkinson, J H, 'Turing's work at the National Physical Laboratory and the Construction of Pilot ACE, DEUCE, and ACE', *A History of Computing in the Twentieth Century* (Academic Press, 1980).

Wilson, Harold, 'Science, Industry and Government', *Nature,* 206, pp230-32 (1965).

Yates, David, *Turing's Legacy: A history of computing at the National Physical Laboratory* (Science Museum, 1993).

'Data Communications at the National Physical Laboratory (1965-1975)', *Annals of the History of Computing,* 9, pp221-247 (1988).

'Government laboratories and the influence of organised Scientists', *Science Studies,* 1, pp331-56 (1971).

'Radiolocation', *Wireless World,* 51, pp66-70 (1965).

'Resources of Science Victorian England: The endowment of science movement, 1868-1900', in Peter Mathias (ed.) *Science and Society 1600-1900,* pp111-66 (Cambridge University Press, 1972).

'Scientists as an Inferior class: The early years of the DSIR', *Minerva,* 8, pp396-411 (1970).

INDEX